LOCAL POLITICS
IN BRITAIN

JOHN GYFORD

CROOM HELM   LONDON

Croom Helm Ltd
2-10 St John's Road, London SW11

ISBN 0-85664-319-X hardback

ISBN 0-85664-475-7 paperback

Printed and bound in Great Britain by
REDWOOD BURN LIMITED
Trowbridge and Esher

CONTENTS

For Janet

PREFACE

This book represents one man's interpretation of the politics of local government. It draws partly on the findings of academic students of the subject and partly on my own experience as, formerly, a local government officer and, latterly, a local politician.

In writing this book I have incurred a number of debts, not least to those writers mentioned in the references in the text. I am especially grateful, though, to Anthony Barker, who first encouraged me to write the book and who offered much helpful advice along the way.

I would also like to thank the Social Science Research Council, whose award of a Senior Research Fellowship for the year 1974-5 enabled me to concentrate full-time on research and writing, and the Department of Government at the University of Essex, for providing a congenial and stimulating working environment.

Thanks are due to all those who agreed to talk to me about their own involvement with local politics, whether in formal interviews or informal conversations. I am also grateful to Mrs. Irene Wagner, of the Labour Party Library, for access to the minutes of the Labour Party National Executive Committee, to Mr Herbert Brabin for access to papers in his possession dealing with the local government work of Conservative Central Office, and to Councillor Dick Wilson for access to certain records of the Labour Party in Nottinghamshire. Finally, my thanks to Carole Lines for her speedy and efficient typing of the manuscript.

None of those mentioned above bear any responsibility for what I have written. If there are any errors of fact or of interpretation in the book, they are mine alone.

John Gyford

1 POLITICS AND LOCAL GOVERNMENT

Traditionally much of the literature about local government has lacked any political dimension. Much of it has been a specialist literature written from within a particular professional perspective, notably that of the lawyer and administrator. The historical nature of local government as a provider of services within a framework of parliamentary legislation no doubt helps to explain the particular character of much of its literature. Moreover it is clearly difficult for any one individual to know many local authorities well simply because they are so numerous. Hence anyone venturing into a generalised account has perhaps been well advised to stick close to those topics where some uniformity of practice is imposed by legal requirement and professional standards. Thus the recurrent topics have been those of areas and functions of local government, of central-local relations, of internal structure and management, and of 'good practice'. This too often imparts a certain aridity to the literature, presenting the dry bones, the skeleton of the institution, but lacking any sense of life or movement.

As a result of this tradition, local government is presented as something which is untainted by problems of political power, by the clash of interests or by the conflict of social groups. Rarely does the literature relate what goes on in local government to any wider social or political trends or to any wider body of knowledge about social processes or political practice in this country or elsewhere.

In the past decade or so the public have shown an increasing awareness that the decisions which issue from their local council are not immaculately conceived. Not only disaffected residents but younger members of local government professions have begun to sense that political questions such as 'who gets what?' can be asked of local, as well as of, central government. As yet however there have been few attempts to describe the workings of local government politics in Britain. There are of course a number of research findings on individual aspects of local politics in selected communities, scattered in a variety of publications. Rarely are they brought together to see how far, and in what way, they might present a composite picture of local politics. This may be in part due to an understandable caution as to how much weight of generalisation the available case studies will bear. Indeed a very wide-ranging survey of political and administrative practice in local authorities, undertaken for the Maud Committee on the Management of Local Government, is notable for the very large number of individual examples which it cites and for the often very tentative nature of the generalisations and observations which it draws from them. (CMLG, 1967, vol.5.)[1]

Nevertheless, an examination of our present knowledge does reveal certain areas of agreement as to what are the big questions and what some of the answers may be. The case studies may not yet be numerous enough nor of adequate scope to allow rigorous generalisation. They can however suggest hypotheses that may prove widely applicable.

To talk of politics in the context of local government is regarded by some as improper; by others as irrelevant. I do not share either of these views which seem to me to arise from a failure to understand the true nature of local government.

In some cases those who abhor the idea of politics in local government are making what is essentially a prescriptive statement — that there ought not to be politics in local government. In the last analysis such a belief clearly depends upon a particular notion of the 'proper' nature of politics and its place in society. Adherents of this view may well concede the relevance of political activity to national issues but draw the line at its incursion on to the local scene. Some critics are of course more specific on the matter, confining their remonstrations to local *party* political activity but this is perhaps to criticise the form rather than the fact of local politics. In any event the issue of party politics in local government is best considered at a later stage, after dealing with the wider issue of politics itself at the local level.

Much of the criticism directed at politics as a facet of local government tends to be expressed in popular but ephemeral terms, in letters to the press, in doorstep conversations or in council debates. It rarely finds expression in the formal literature. Underlying many expressions of this viewpoint there seems to be, at bottom, a desire to see the local community as a community at one with itself, agreed on doing 'what is best for the town', and not riven by the clash of interests or ideas. In practice such generalised notions of the good of the community are rarely made specific; certainly they are rarely operationalised in such a way as to make them useful as guides to action. Various interpretations may be placed upon the calls for policies that benefit the local community as a whole. They may be construed as seeking policies that benefit everybody in the community, or that benefit a majority, or that benefit those most affected by a particular issue. What seems generally to underly the appeal for an a-political form of local government is the desire for a community founded on consensus rather than conflict, no matter how vaguely that consensus may be defined. It is of course true that ever since the Industrial Revolution generations of Englishmen have indulged in a nostalgic love affair with a somewhat idyllic interpretation of pre-Industrial community life wherein the villagers, from the highest to the lowest, lived at one with each other and engaged in the common tasks of village life. Certainly the recurring appeal of the image of the united small-scale community can be seen throughout our modern history, from the writings of Ebenezer Howard, prophet of the Garden City, and, in a different vein, George Orwell, to the recent success of Ronald Blythe's *Akenfield* and the desire of the mobile middle class to escape to the 'real' community life of their dreams in a weekend country cottage. In the context of local government this attitude expresses itself as a desire that everybody in the community should 'pull together' and engage, not in the promotion of sectional or selfish interests or the debating of ideals, but in the search for whatever is 'best for Barchester'.

It is scarcely surprising that those who cherish the notion of a consensual approach to local affairs should abhor any form of politicisation of local government. Definitions of politics tend to stress that it is concerned with conflict and disagreement. If conflict and disagreement were absent we would not need to talk of politics. Instead we could rely on administration or management to solve local problems.

In practice it is as true locally as it is nationally that 'politics arises in the first instance when one realises that there is no such thing as *the* people — that no single decision can please all people. There are only *peoples,* with contradictory and conflicting ideas and interests.' (Bell and Held, 1969, p.177.) Here we encounter the notion that politics arises from the lack of identity of ideas and interests amongst the population of a community. This is of course merely another way of formulating the politician's old saying that you can't please all the people all the time. Given the fact of limited resources certain decisions about their allocation mean that some people will win and others will lose. A simple example illustrates the point. Proposals for an improved road scheme for a small town offered two options. One involved a new road cutting across a park and recreation ground to the detriment of sportsmen and users of the park. As against this an alternative road line could be secured by cutting across an area of housing to the detriment of local residents. Whichever line was chosen somebody was bound to lose and this could not be obscured by dressing the issue up in terms of public interest. In the event the dilemma was resolved by simply abandoning the road scheme entirely. This was obviously to the benefit of the groups previously mentioned but to the detriment of the residents and shopkeepers in the congested High Street who could have benefited had one or other variant of the scheme been implemented.

Another definition of politics worth noting is that by Rose to the effect that politics is concerned with 'the regulation of disagreements about matters of public choice' (Rose, 1974a, p.282). As Dearlove notes however, there are no objective criteria by which one can identify a public problem in the sense of a problem requiring a governmental solution (Dearlove, 1973, p.211). Hence disagreement can extend to the identification, as well as the resolution, of matters of public choice. Thus for example there would be little agreement as to the proper range of local government activity between a Conservative such as Sherman who would like to see many present municipal functions contracted out to private enterprise (Sherman, 1970, p.132) and a Socialist like Dixey who hopes that 'municipal enterprise, community development and Socialism will advance along the same broad front' (Dixey, 1974, p.16).

If it be accepted that there can be conflicts as to what are the local public problems and choices of the day, that there may be 'peoples' within a community who have differing views and objectives, and that the resolution of the consequent disagreements is the stuff of politics, then it is hard to escape the conclusion that in some form there must be political activity in a local community and that some of this activity must be directed towards and enacted within the local organs of government.

The question may still be asked however as to what is the nature of the politics to be found in local government. To what conflicts does it address itself? Expanding slightly on a scheme of Wildavsky (1966, p.306) we may identify four types of politics. 'Policy politics' concerns the question of which policy will be adopted. 'Partisan politics' concerns the matter of which party will win a given contest (be it an election or a debate). 'System politics' deals with the issue of what structures and procedures are instituted in order to produce decisions. 'Patronage politics' deals with the distribution of individual (or group) assignments to posts within the decision making system.

In practice most observers of local government would admit that partisan, system and patronage politics do occur. Elections and debates are held and won or lost, committee structures and standing orders are established and revised, chairmanships and other appointments are given and taken away. However, these activities are arguably subordinate to the ultimate aim of adopting or rejecting solutions to public problems – policy politics.

Now although conflicts over issues of partisan, system and patronage politics may be recognised as existing there are some who would argue that it is unrealistic to talk of local policy politics. Here we encounter those for whom politics in local government is not improper or undesirable so much as an irrelevance. They argue not that it ought not to exist but that at least as far as policy issues are concerned, it cannot be said to exist at all.

This line of argument rests on the proposition that local authorities have little discretion as to what policy decisions they take because they are not free agents but are effectively mere tools of the central government. Thus for example Cole asserted that 'the business of local government is primarily administration – that is to say it is concerned with the execution of laws passed by Parliament or of functions conferred by ancient Charters' (Cole, 1947, p.29) whilst to Dell 'the central government's victory over local democracy is complete. . .Local Government today is little more than a part of an administrative machine whose policy it can no longer significantly influence' (Dell, 1960, p.235). Other commentators have made similar observations – for example, Green (1959, p.156), Jackson (1965, p.275) and Robson (1966, p.67) – whilst both the Maud Committee and the Wheatley Commission identified a tendency for control and direction by the central government to increase and Maud feared that this could 'weaken local government as an organ of government and detract from its effectiveness' (CMLG, 1967, vol.1, p.76; RCLGS, 1969, Report, p.30).[2] In Dell's graphic phrase the argument is that 'the Town Hall is merely the local administrative office of the Government' (Dell, 1960, p.237).

As Dearlove points out the most frequently cited explanation for the subservience of local authorities is their growing reliance upon central finance. Another possible factor is the desire to ensure nationwide uniformity of provision in the Welfare State so that people receive equal standards of service no matter where they live (Dearlove, 1973, pp.12-13). It is certainly the case that on paper at least the central government has many powerful weapons at its command if it wishes to bring local authorities to heel in some way (Griffith, 1966). But as Dearlove points out there has been little attempt, for example, to relate the degree of effective control over authorities and their services to the extent of dependence on central finance. (Dearlove, 1973, p.13). From an examination of county boroughs and administrative counties, Ashford has concluded that 'the heavy financial dependance of British local authorities on central government has not produced a demonstrable effect on policy choice' and that 'several of the more emotional arguments about central dominance of local affairs are exaggerated, if not totally incorrect' (Ashford, 1974, p.320). One possible explanation for the light touch of the national government's supposedly heavy hand is offered by Poole when he points out that 'authorities are free to use rate support grants as they think fit within the compass of their statutory functions. . .loan sanction is a negative rather than a positive weapon. . .Judicial review in particular is beset by procedural pitfalls . . .larger authorities in particular are able to finance some capital development out of revenue, thus avoiding the loan sanction procedure . . .reserve statutory powers (e.g. default, withholding grant, giving directions in particular instances) are rarely used and exist largely *in terrorem* and their effectiveness as such is necessarily an unknown quantity. . . (Poole, 1970, pp.11-12).

Moreover, in their relations with local authorities government departments may use differing combinations of advice, exhortation, promotion and inspection (Griffith, 1966, p.515) with greater or lesser degrees of effectiveness. The limitations to which some of these strategies are subject are explored by Dearlove in the case of Kensington and Chelsea. He examined the reaction of the Royal Borough to Ministerial advice and direction on such issues as the appointment of an architect at chief officer level, the introduction of parking meters, the imposition of council house rent increases and the acquisition of land for public open space. His finding was that the actions of the borough in going contrary to Ministerial wishes on these issues showed that it was 'prepared to stand out against the advice and direction contained in government White Papers, circulars, private meetings with Ministers, and personal letters'. He concluded from these cases that 'the impact of central government upon the day-to-day decisions of local authorities often depends on local responsiveness, and the preparedness of local authorities to accept advice or guidance which in law the central government has no strict authority to give and no legal power to enforce' (Dearlove, 1973, p.20).

Instead of taking the narrow view that sees central government as a prime mover and local government as a mere agent, we would do well to recognise that in their workings all governments at all levels are

constrained by a variety of factors. The government of Britain is
constrained in its actions by various legal, political, financial and moral
obligations to other governments and to international bodies and
groupings, by the availability of resources, and by the accepted norms of
the nation's political culture. The key questions relate to how far
governments are inhibited by these restraints from following policies
which they regard as appropriate to their particular circumstances. If
local government were truly hobbled by centrally imposed constraints
we would expect this to be revealed in the experience of local
politicians. There is certainly little evidence that local government
officers and councillors feel unduly hampered by central controls. In
their research for the Maud Committee Harrison and Norton found that
'less than half the members and officers interviewed felt that central
controls were generally unreasonable and very few felt strongly on the
matter' (CMLG, 1967, vol.5, p.534). As for the supposedly restrictive
effect of the *ultra vires* rule 'the number of members and officers who
were not conscious that it exercised any inhibiting effect surprised us.
Some insisted that there was always a way round the law if one looked
hard enough.' (CMLG, 1967, vol.5, p.449.) This attitude on the part of
those involved in local government is of course open to more than one
interpretation. It may be the case that even on a narrow construction
of their freedom of action some authorities find themselves stretched to
the limit in relation to available resources. If they are thus hard pressed
to fulfil minimal statutory obligations they are hardly likely to worry
about whether or not there are other things they could be doing as well.
Alternatively, it might be the case that councillors and officers have
become so used to constraints that they are scarcely conscious of them
and thus do not worry over them. A third interpretation is that the
attitudes noted by Harrison and Norton can be taken at face value, and
that in practice local government does not feel unduly confined by the
legal and financial powers of central government. It should be
remembered that those who choose to serve in local government,
whether as officers or as elected members, and those who look to local
government for provision of services, have somewhat more modest
aspirations than many of their counterparts at Westminster. They do
not aspire to shape the destiny of nations through foreign policy, nor
to remodel the structure of the national economy. They seek to
provide a certain range of public services over a given geographical area
in a manner tolerably consistent with notions of democracy. The
amount of room to manoeuvre which they require in order to perform
this task according to their lights may be quite modest. This may in

turn explain the apparent lack of any sense of being subject to undue restrictions from the centre.

Central government is not of course the only possible source of restrictions on local autonomy. Even if, in practice, central government allows local authorities a certain room for manoeuvre the councillors concerned might still be hobbled by constraints from another central body — the political party headquarters. If the national headquarters of the parties sought to impose a uniform party line on all their councillors this would clearly prevent the enjoyment of such local autonomy as central government allows, at least on those councils, now increasing as a proportion of the whole, where party politicians are in control. The Maud Committee stated that they had 'no evidence to show to what extent party groups of a local authority accept guidance or instructions from national party headquarters' (CMLG, 1967, vol.1, para.380, pp.111-2). Given the growing importance of party in local politics (*see* Chapter 3 below) it is clearly of some consequence to try and establish whether party politics on local councils entails some form of remote control of councillors from party headquarters.

It is certainly the case that national party managers have long taken an interest in local politics. Initially however this interest was focused on local election results as portents of likely trends in national public opinion, rather than on the workings of local councils as such (Hanham, 1959, p.389). The first attempt by a national party to intervene centrally in substantive issues of local government seems to have been the creation of a Local Government Information Bureau, set up following a conference of Independent Labour Party councillors in 1899 and run jointly by the ILP and the Fabian Society (Pease, 1963, p.206). The emphasis in this intervention was on informing and assisting councillors rather than on controlling their activities, and this has remained true of all subsequent local government work at national party headquarters, be they Labour, Liberal or Conservative.

Labour has the longest tradition of central party involvement in local government work. After the First World War the party established a Local Government Advisory Committee to advise party officials and MPs on local government affairs; it considered issues such as rating, municipal banking, housing finance, payment of councillors, and local government reform (Labour Party NEC Minutes: Local Government Advisory Committee 1918-1922, Memoranda Nos. 1-60). This body however seems to have dwindled into inactivity during the 1920s (Robson, 1931). It was replaced in 1932 by a Local Government Sub-Committee of the Policy Committee of the Party's National

Executive (Labour Party NEC Minutes, Oct. 1931-Jan. 1932 and Jan.-Feb. 1932), a body which has persisted in varying incarnations to the present day. Its membership has varied from time to time, and currently includes leading Labour councillors from the local authority associations, other co-opted councillors, one member from each of the Party's regional councils, plus NEC members, MPs and Ministers. The main purpose of the Committee now is to act as a sounding board for municipal Labour reaction to central government proposals, and to discuss new policy ideas.[3] Occasionally it has suggested resolutions which Labour Groups might care to move in their local councils but it has no means of making them do so.

Another sub-committee of Labour's NEC also finds itself involved in local government — the Organisation Sub-Committee. This body deals with internal organisational and procedural disputes within the party. Recently some two-thirds of the forty or fifty disputes which reach the sub-committee each year, not having been resolved at Regional Office level, have had their origin in local government (Cartwright and Underhill Interviews). They arise mainly in relation to conflicts over local election candidacies, over party group discipline on the council, and over relations between the party, the group, and the individual councillor, and are often the product of personality, ambition, poor organisation, and poor communication rather than of ideology or policy disputes. The function of the sub-committee in such cases is to ensure that correct procedures according to the party's constitution have been followed. As such it is concerned largely with the relationships between and within local party branches and party groups, rather than with relations between the national party and the local councillors.

The fact is that neither constitutionally nor in practicality is Transport House able to control the actions of Labour councillors according to some single national party line. The two sub-committees already mentioned are responsible to the NEC, which is responsible in turn to Annual Conference. Councillors are not responsible to the NEC or to the Annual Conference, but to their local party branches. There is in fact no constitutional link or mechanism whereby either Conference or the NEC could impose its will on party branches and local councillors so long as their policies — whatever they may be — are made according to the correct procedures laid down in the party's rules. Thus no attempt was — or could have been — made by Conference to instruct Labour councillors how to act on such an issue as the Housing Finance Act of 1972 despite the strong views of Conference itself.

In practical terms the question of central control over local policy

making was aptly disposed of over forty years ago following a dispute
in West Ham, when the NEC accepted that 'the policy of a Labour
Group on a local authority is local in character and has to be decided
upon local circumstances' and that 'time would not permit of
reference to Head Office of matters upon the agenda of local authorities'
(Labour Party NEC Minutes, October, 1932). Given the shortage of
staff — a Local Government Department of two people — and the
practical impossibility of monitoring every Labour Group's activities,
central Labour party control over its councillors is simply not a feasible
proposition.

On the Conservative side central party involvement dates back only
to the appraisal of party policy and organisation under R.A. Butler
which began towards the end of the Second World War. One of the
results was the establishment of an Advisory Committee on Local
Government which met for the first time in 1944 (Hoffman, 1964,
p.62) and the creation of a Local Government Department at
Conservative Central Office in 1946.

The Department was set up with the aim of 'assisting Conservative
councillors and workers to be well informed on all aspects of local
government' but with 'no intention that there should be direction on
general policy' (Conservative Party, 1958, p.185; Conservative Central
Office Circular quoted in *Manchester Guardian,* 14 August 1946).
Accordingly it operates mainly as an information and advice centre
advising on policy, offering legal guidance and limited technical help,
and keeping councillors and national politicians in touch with each
other. The present head of the department has described it as basically
a 'communications centre' (Allen Interview) and as such its function
resembles that of its opposite number at Transport House, as does its
modest size — two staff plus secretarial assistance.

The National Local Government Advisory Committee draws its
membership from the party's Area Advisory Committees on Local
Government, from the Conservative leaders on the major authorities
(including the six Metropolitan Counties, twenty non-metropolitan
counties, the GLC and the six largest cities), and from other sources
such as the Young Conservatives and Conservative MPs. Its function is
purely one of presenting advice to the executive of the National Union
of Conservative and Unionist Associations on local government matters,
and it has no executive powers of its own either at central or at local
level. It certainly has no power over individual Conservative councillors
or Groups. Unlike the Labour Party the Conservatives have no
constitutional provision which enables local procedural disputes to be

appealed upwards from constituency through area level to party
headquarters. Thus there is no institution at Central Office akin to
Labour's Organisation Sub-Committee concerned with untangling
municipal rivalries amongst local politicians, although there may be the
occasional offer of informal assistance from the Local Government
Department if a problem cannot be readily resolved at Area Central
Office (Allen Interview). In this sense Central Office is freed from a
burden which Transport House itself has found rather onerous. Recent
revisions of Labour Party rules have attempted to reduce the number
of municipal disputes coming up to party headquarters by making the
Regional Councils the final court of appeal in certain instances (Labour
Party, 1975), and it seems clear that Labour's NEC has no particular
relish for the task hitherto imposed on it by the party constitution in
this respect.

It is apparent that both in the Labour and Conservative parties there
are neither the constitutional mechanisms, nor the resources, nor the
inclination to permit the effective central control of the parties' local
councillors. The main thrust of central party involvement in local
government is in the fields of discussion and consultation on present
and projected policies, in the provision of information and advice
through study groups, publications and conferences, and in servicing
the party groups on the three national local authority associations
which are increasingly recognised as important links between the local
and national party politicians. There is no attempt to lay down any
single party line to be obeyed by party councillors everywhere regardless
of local circumstance.

If we examine in broad terms the actual performance of local
authorities the picture that emerges is by no means one of rigid
constraint, and certainly lends little credence to the notion that local
government is used effectively to secure a uniform provision of services
nationwide. Various writers have pointed out, for example, the wide
differences in expenditure per head on such services as education, social
services, health, housing, libraries, and fire and police protection.
(Boaden, 1970 and 1971b; Boaden and Alford, 1969; Oliver and
Stanyer, 1969: Alt, 1971; Davies, B. 1968). From his own studies
Boaden draws the conclusion that 'the range of expenditure is very
wide in each of the services which tends to contradict the concentration
of standards implicit in central control' (Boaden, 1970, pp.180-1). In
the case of individual services similar conclusions have been drawn. The
Seebohm Committee concluded that 'local authority personal social
services are not fully meeting needs for which, on the basis of the duties

placed on them by statutes, they are clearly responsible. . .comparative statistics. . .indicate considerable differences in the quality of services provided in different areas'. Moreover 'Such unevenness does not bear any systematic relationship to differences in local need'. (CLAPSS, 1968, paras.74-5.)[4] Douglas has noted the variations that exist in educational opportunities between different local authorities (Douglas, 1964, pp.1-2), whilst the varying pace of movement towards comprehensive secondary education as between one authority and another is widely known. In the field of housing variations have been observed in the scale of capital investment (Nicholson and Topham, 1972). In the case of child care Lees states that 'many authorities went beyond the duties and powers conferred upon them by the Children's Act of 1948 to receive children into care, and undertook intensive casework. . .before the passing of the Children and Young Person's Act, 1963' (Lees, 1972, p.58).

Thus there seems to be, in practice considerable scope for a local authority to make its own interpretation of the duties and opportunities bequeathed it by central government. 'Between the minimum of services which must be provided and the maximum which a council may not exceed, there is a wide area of discretion.' (Redcliffe-Maud and Wood, 1974, p.19.) However, this area of discretion should not be seen merely in terms of spending more or less on prescribed services. This would be to minimise the ability of local councils to make innovations in the range and format of services they offer. Thus Cossey points to local authorities who have made individual innovations in such fields as establishing advice centres for housing, planning and the consumer; free birth control; free bus travel for pensioners; tenant management in housing; establishing neighbourhood councils; pedestrianisation of streets; and reclamation of canals and railway lines for recreation (Cossey, 1974, p.17). Other initiatives include such ventures as the village colleges in Cambridgeshire, the new towns of Killingworth and Cramlington in Northumberland (both joint County-District undertakings), and the provision of free television licenses for pensioners at Clay Cross. The last example provides an instance of the imaginative use of existing legislation, in this case the 1948 National Assistance Act with its provision for local authority spending on recreation for pensioners (Mitchell, 1974, p.177). Other examples of imaginative use of statutes have included the provision of a public toilet under open space legislation and of a car park under the Burial Acts (Morton, 1970). As a last resort for the authority determined to go its own way there is always the possibility of simple (even if

unlawful) evasion of central government requirements. Thus one
authority disagreed with the regulations governing both the lowest age
for admission to secondary school and the need for nursery school
children to attend two sessions a day. As a result these regulations were
'quietly evaded' (Kogan, 1973, p.167).

How far a local council is prepared to experiment and innovate and
develop its own priorities as best it can is very much a question of
political temperament and willpower. Some councils will be guided by
the philosophy of Herbert Morrison who instructed the Solicitor to the
London County Council thus: 'I don't want to know why I can't do
this. Tell me how I can.' (Donoughue and Jones, 1973, p.195.) Other
councils will take a more cautious line and will rarely attempt anything
beyond the familiar round.

Evidence and experience thus seems to suggest that local authorities
do have room to manoeuvre within the limits laid down by legislation,
and that they have scope for decision making about levels and types of
expenditure and provision which enables them to exercise some degree
of autonomous power within their own geographical boundaries.
Moreover, although the precise degree of autonomy may seem small
when viewed at Whitehall 'from the top down' it may loom much
larger when seen 'from the bottom up'. Thus when Lees argues that 'it
is clear that crucial policy decisions are taken by local authorities' (Lees,
1972, p.55) he is right in the sense that councils are taking decisions
crucial to those they serve locally. Decisions such as whether or not to
accept metropolitan overspill, or to abandon a road scheme, or to
subsidise bus fares, or to retain corporal punishment in schools may be
minor decisions in the terms of Westminster, but can have an
immediate importance to local inhabitants. The ability to make
autonomous decisions on these and other issues is of some consequence
at the bottom of the political system, if not necessarily at the top.

If it is accepted that local authorities are not merely rubber
stamping the edicts of Westminster, but can and do make locally
significant policy decisions of their own, then of course one could say
that policy politics is indeed found within local government, along with
partisan, system and patronage politics. Even then, however, some
might argue that in fact the policy decisions that have to be taken at
local level are in some way technical rather than political decisions.
According to this school of thought there is no room for controversy
over such questions as the best way to surface a road or empty a
dustbin.

However, this view of local policy decisions perhaps owes too much to the historic legacy of the days when local government was mainly involved in exercises in municipal housekeeping such as street cleaning, lighting, paving, drainage and sewerage, refuse disposal and policing. These activities may indeed be reducible to questions of technique and value for money and may not give rise to much local debate. Even so it may be noted that modest problems of paving and lighting have become the stock in trade of some local politicians eager to ferret out those minor civic aggravations which the citizen normally endures in resigned silence, whilst the collection — or non-collection — of refuse has been a lively issue in both London and Glasgow in recent years. Nevertheless one might concede that these local government functions are those least likely to give rise to major controversy over policy. Yet municipal housekeeping has long since ceased to be the sole, or even the prime, function of local government.

During the present century local authorities have acquired a number of functions in fields such as housing, planning, education, social services, transportation and consumer protection. These have in common the fact that policies adopted in respect of them can have consequences for the life-styles and life-chances of local residents. Decisions made in these policy areas are more than decisions about technique and good husbandry, and are increasingly recognised as such. For example the assessment and selection of secondary school children at the age of eleven, although once regarded simply as a technical issue for teachers and administrators, is now seen as being equally a political issue involving councillors and parents. This is because it has been recognised as having major implications for the future lives, beyond school, of the children concerned. Similarly the development of housing estates can no longer be seen as purely a question of density, layout, dwelling types and form of tenure (owner-occupier or council tenant) because each of these ostensibly technical or financial considerations has implications in terms of the types of people to be housed and the impact they make on the way of life of already established residents. In the field of planning it is increasingly recognised that planners are not merely designing the 'city beautiful' but are distributing spatial resources, notably 'the control of place in time' (Williams, 1971, p.12) with important social consequences for the lives of different groups within the community (Pahl, 1970; Simmie, 1974). Even in the case of transportation, which might be seen as essentially a technical matter, it is clear that varying mixes of transport provision can impose differential costs and benefits on various social groups, to the extent that in the United States the term 'the transportation poor' has been coined to describe those groups whose way of life is adversely affected by their enforced immobility.

It is thus clear that at the local level questions of policy can arise whose resolution may have varying consequences for different groups within a given community. The reactions of these groups to the likelihood of their being beneficially or adversely affected by such decisions imparts a political dimension to the decision making process. To return once more to Rose's definition of politics we find ourselves confronting the necessity for 'the regulation of disagreements about matters of public choice' (Rose, 1974a, p.282).

Once it is accepted that politics exist at the local as well as at the national level then it is logical to anticipate that this politics will express itself through some form of local political system. In defining the nature of that system however, we encounter a problem that does not arise at the national level. A political system can be defined as 'a set of structures and processes, the core of which is an authoritative centre of decision making' (Cox and Morgan, 1973, p.21). In the national context the constitutional supremacy of a sovereign Parliament has enabled easy identification of just such an authoritative centre, in that ultimately all powers of public authority within the boundaries of the United Kingdom have their source in Parliament. The same type of situation cannot be said to exist within the boundaries of a local authority. A local council may well be an authoritative centre of decision making in those matters remitted (by Parliament) to its charge, but on other matters there will be equally authoritative local decisions emanating from such sources as the local offices of central government departments, statutory undertakings, and nationalised industries. If we were to attempt a comprehensive picture of what one writer calls 'territorial government' (Bulpitt, 1972, p.297) we should need to expand our analysis beyond local councils to the various field agencies of central government and other public bodies operating within the territorial boundaries of local authorities. However, the concern of this book is solely with the political system whose core is the formal institution of local government. This system embraces those 'individuals, groups and institutions who seek to influence how (local) government works' (Rose, 1974a, p.17). It is to the component parts of this system that we must now direct our attention.

At a minimum these component parts clearly include the officials, the councillors and the electors. In terms of political practice, however, experience shows that the list must be extended to include, for example, political parties, pressure groups, and the media, all of whom at various times seek some influence over local government and its workings.

Notes

1. CMLG – Committee on the Management of Local Government.
2. RCLGS – Royal Commission on Local Government in Scotland. Kellas (1975, p.143) suggests that perhaps the Scottish Office exercises rather more central control than do the English government departments.
3. In dealing with policy questions, the sub-committee has to cope with the problem that some of the policy areas relevant to local government also come within the remit of other NEC sub-committees, e.g. housing, town and country planning, etc.

   In conveying municipal Labour reaction to Labour government proposals, the sub-committee is not the only channel. The political advisors of some individual Labour Ministers also have their own municipal contacts.
4. CLAPSS – Committee on Local Authority and Allied Personal Social Services.

2 INSIDE THE TOWN HALL

The core of the local government political system is the local authority
itself, incarnate in the form of the Town (or County, or City) Hall and
the officers and councillors who work within it. In strict legal terms the
relationship between these two sets of individuals is quite clear. The
officers, individually, are the appointed employees of the elected
councillors as a corporate body. The councillors, again as a corporate
body rather than as individuals, are vested with the powers and duties
of making decisions in the name of authority. The officers are employed
to assist councillors in arriving at their decisions and to put those
decisions into operation. However, behind these simple formulations
there is a more complex reality. This reality owes its nature to the
characteristics, the dispositions, the perceptions and the resources of the
two groups as well as to the constitutional structures within which they
operate.

The Elected Members

There are now some 23,500 councillors in Britain (with the exclusion
of parish and community councillors). These 23,500 individuals have in
common their ability to meet the legal requirements that they should
be aged twenty-one or over, be either an occupant of premises (or land)
or a worker in the area of the local authority for at least twelve months,
and not be an employee of the local authority. Their other characteristics
are likely to be more varied. Unfortunately, we lack detailed information
on the social characteristics of councillors on the new authorities which
came into being after local government reorganisation. However, the
findings of the 1964-5 investigations for the Maud Committee and the
Wheatley Commission[1] give us a useful bench-mark against which to
make some observations on the current situation.

   The Maud Committee found English and Welsh councillors to be on
average much older than the general population, with more than half
the male councillors being over the age of 55. Only one councillor in
eight was a woman (CMLG, 1967, vol.2, table 1.1). In terms of social
origins the manual workers were very under-represented as councillors
in proportion to their share of the total population whilst employers,
farmers and managers of small businesses were much over-represented
(CMLG, 1967, vol.2, table 1.7). Councillors were likely to have had a

more extensive education than the average citizen and some 15 per cent
of them had had some form of further education (CMLG, 1967, vol.2,
Table 1.14). Scottish councillors had similar social characteristics.
Women were even less well represented north of the border, accounting
for less than one Scottish councillor in ten (RCLGS, 1969, Appendix
25). These figures may in fact represent something of an
underestimation of the bias in the social composition of local councils.
They are based on information gathered at a time when Labour had
enjoyed a fairly good run of local election results during 1962, 1963
and 1964 and to that extent may not truly indicate the low extent of
working-class membership on councils under other political conditions.

This cautionary note indicates that the make-up of a council in
social terms may be partly a reflection of political complexion. There is
evidence that councils with strong Labour representation are likely to
have a higher than average proportion of working-class councillors. Even
then, however, unskilled manual workers are likely to remain
unrepresented. There has been historically a tendency for a slight
decline in the proportion of older upper-class males amongst councillors,
along with a corresponding increase in younger men and women from
the lower middle class and skilled working class. This may be due to
the growth in Labour strength and also to a widening of the social bases
of recruitment by local Conservative parties (Sharpe, 1962b; Morris and
Newton, 1971). As far as Labour councillors are concerned there is
some indication that they are likely to have risen in the social scale,
from manual working-class jobs to positions as trade union officials and
insurance agents for example (Rees and Smith, 1964; Brand 1973).
This could explain the phenomenom that not even councils with strong
Labour majorities will necessarily show a majority of councillors from
manual occupations, even on the Labour benches alone (Hampton,
1970, p.189).

The Maud Committed attached some importance to the motion that
all sections of the community should be adequately represented in local
government, in order that first-hand knowledge and experience from all
quarters might be brought to bear on local problems (CMLG, 1967,
vol.2, pp.2 and 7). It is doubtful whether the new local authorities will
come any nearer this goal than did their predecessors. The experience
of local government reorganisation in Greater London in the 1960s
may be something of a guide to what happens when local authorities
are recast into larger units. Thus the councillors elected to the new
London Borough of Camden in 1964 contained a higher proportion of
owner-occupiers, professional men, and those with some further

education, than did the membership of the smaller outgoing
Metropolitan Borough Councils (Wistrich, 1972, p.70). This would
suggest, albeit tentatively, that the introduction of larger authorities
may lead to increasing representation on the council of the professional
middle class and skilled working class at the expense of other groups in
the community.

The consequences of reorganisation outside Greater London are not
yet wholly clear in this respect. Reorganisation was certainly the
occasion for the retirement, voluntary or enforced, of a number of
elderly councillors. It may therefore be the case that the new councils
began life with a rather lower average age amongst their members than
had their predecessors. This could however, prove to be a passing
change if the new members remain in office and grow old together. The
increased geographical size of the new authorities will make greater
demands on councillors in terms of time and travelling and this may
reduce recruitment from some sources, perhaps especially from amongst
manual workers in the private sector who find difficulty in securing the
necessary time. It is certainly true that the percentage of women on
the new county councils is no higher than on the old (Bristow, 1975).
Hill suggests that increasingly the new counties will tend to attract the
younger, better-educated, more middle-class members, with interests in
major issues of long-term policy, with the older, more working-class
councillors being confined to local issues at the district level (Hill, D.M.,
1974, p.213). All in all the chances of achieving a representative cross
section of the community amongst members of the new authorities do
not seem very good.

The social composition of a local council will be affected by the
methods used to recruit its members, and also by the motivations
which drive some people rather than others to seek public office. The
Maud Committee found that about a third of all councillors were
initially brought into touch with council work, or asked to stand for
election, by the political parties. The political parties, and the trade
unions, were especially important avenues of recruitment for manual
workers. Just over a third of councillors were invited to stand by private
people or in other informal ways (CMLG, 1967, vol.2, pp.59-61). In
terms of specific reasons for deciding to stand the main factors were a
desire to remedy a particular situation, to plead a particular cause, or
simply to live up to an ideal of social service. None of the councillors
surveyed mentioned purely political reasons for standing such as an
interest in politics or political ambition (CMLG, 1967, vol.2, table
2.21).

Once on the council, continued membership clearly depends — voters willing — on deriving satisfaction from the work involved. In fact for many councillors their work on the council is more satisfying than their normal daily occupation: notably, nearly two-thirds of manual worker councillors expressed this view (CMLG 1967, vol.2, table 4.13). The aspects of council work most likely to give satisfaction were housing, old people's welfare and education rather than general across-the-board policy making (CMLG, 1967, vol.2, table 4.1). Whatever the source of satisfaction it was felt by three out of four councillors that their work as a councillor enabled them to use abilities which would otherwise have lain dormant (CMLG, 1967, vol.2, table 4.9). There are perhaps also more intangible reasons why councillors persist in their membership. Harrison and Norton noted that some members seemed to see the council as some form of club, and it is certainly the case that the prime quality that councillors sought in one another were the 'clubable' virtues of broadmindedness, patience, sense of humour, impartiality, pleasant personality and an ability to mix and talk (CMLG, 1967, vol.5, p.38, and vol.2, table 2.27). Other observers have noticed this phenomenon. Headrick commented that despite class or party divisions 'it is just as if the council were a club and there were a set of unwritten rules which every member of the club religiously observed', whilst Rees and Smith found that 'the Town Hall is the best club in Barking' (Headrick, 1962, p.80; Rees and Smith, 1964, p.79). There would thus seem to be good reasons of sociability, social service, and an intrinsic satisfaction with the work to explain why councillors should wish to stay in office once elected. As against these attractions there must be set the factors leading to voluntary withdrawal from the council. Apart from old age and ill-health, the major reasons were inability, or unwillingness, to devote adequate time, and domestic and/or business pressures. Although on average about 6 per cent of councillors gave up their council work each year the turnover rate varied with manual workers tending to stay on longer than professional people or managers and employers in large firms. Turnover was also especially high amongst the younger age groups, the better educated and the self-employed (CMLG, 1967, vol.2, tables 9.3, 9.5, 9.13, 9.22 and vol.5, pp.49-50).

Under the re-organised structure of local government it seems likely that the responsibility for maintaining the membership of councils will devolve increasingly on the political parties as they expand their activities into previously non-party areas. This renders all the more important the ways in which local parties go about securing candidates and we shall examine this more fully in the next chapter.

Once elected it is open to the councillor to pursue his duties in a variety of ways. Thus the Bains Report suggested that members might aim to perform any of five different tasks: taking broad policy decisions, engaging in welfare activities for constituents, 'managing' the authority often on commercial principles, serving the community in the general sense, and controlling and limiting spending (Department of the Environment, 1972b, para.3.8). Similarly, Jones estimates that broadly councillors fall into three main groups with 75 per cent being chiefly concerned with representing ward and constituents' interests, 20 per cent being policy makers in a special service area such as housing or education, and 5 per cent being involved with general authority-wide policy making (Jones, 1973a, p.142). Although both these observations are true as far as they go, they fail to separate out clearly the different facets of the councillor's role. In executing his role the councillor has a number of options available to him in terms of how he performs in relation not merely towards his constituents, or towards the workload of the local authority, but also towards his party (if any), the local pressure groups, the officers, and the community outside his particular ward. A number of attempts have been made to investigate and to summarise the wide variety of role orientations which a councillor may assume, notably by Newton (1974b), Budge and his colleagues (1972), Dearlove (1973), Lee (1963), Heclo (1969), and McKinsey and Co. (1973). One general conclusion which does emerge from the various studies is that the choice of role orientations by councillors is not primarily associated with age, sex or social class, but rather with such factors as seniority and length of service on the council, the character of the councillor's ward, and his party political allegiance. Moreover, many of these orientations are apparently linked one with another, forming as it were 'clusters' which provide differing emphases to the varying aspects of a councillor's role. A graphical presentation of these orientations, and their development through a councillor's career is seen in Fig.1. This diagram brings together a number of findings about specific aspects of the councillor's role and attempts to relate them to each other. The columns show:

Column 1: Status, Senior or Junior, refers to the councillor's length of service and also to the nature of that service, e.g. as back-bencher or chairman of a committee or officer of a party group.

Column 2: Ward Type distinguishes between wards where the incumbent may anticipate re-election and those where the contest is highly competitive.

Figure 1: The Role of the Councillor

	1	2	3	4	5	6	7	8	9	10	11	12	13
	Status	Ward Type	Style	Focus	Relations with Constituents	Relations with Interest Groups	Issue Orientation	Form of Involvement	Relations with Officers	Information Sources	Information Actions	Political Views	Political Behaviour
Tribune	Junior	Marginal	Delegate	Ward	Welfare Officer	Facilitator and Spokesman	General	Casework	Watchdog	Internal and External	Search	Ideological	Maverick
			Politico	Ward and Community	Commun-icator		Specific						
Statesman	Senior	Safe	Trustee	Community	Mentor	Resistor and Referee	General	Policy	Colleague	Internal	Wait	Admin-istrative	Loyalist

Column 3: Style refers to the manner in which the councillor relates his own views to those he represents. The trustee is one who relies on his own sense of what is correct and just, the delegate accepts a mandate from his constituents regardless of his own views, whilst the politico may either adopt a combination of the other two styles or alternate between them (Eulau *et al.*, 1959, pp.749-51).

Column 4: 'Focus' distinguishes between the two communities to which the councillor owes his loyalties, the smaller unit of the ward or the larger local community as a whole.

Column 5: Distinguishes between three ways of serving constituents — the 'welfare officer' helping out with their problems; the communicator keeping them informed about official plans and proposals; and the mentor giving a lead on the issues of the day (Wahlke *et al.*, 1962, pp.304-8).

Column 6: In terms of dealing with local pressure groups, the councillor may befriend them, facilitate their access to authority, and even act as their spokesman, or conversely resist them, keep them at arms length, and adjudicate between their demands on the basis of his own perceptions of the public good.

Columns 7, 8 & 9: These have to do with the distinction between checking decisions and making decisions: some councillors will act as watchdogs over the officers, taking up individual problems, over a wide range of policy areas: others, after perhaps a period of single-service policy making, will be working with the officers on across-the-board policy issues in the role Lee (1963) calls the public person.

Columns 10 & 11: These refer to how the councillor goes about acquiring his information, some of them searching it out often from external sources, others waiting for information from the official machine (Dearlove, 1973, ch.9).

Finally, *Columns 12 & 13* refer to the ideological zeal of the councillor and his degree of loyalty to party decisions.

In setting out the development of role orientations in adjoining columns in this way it is not being suggested that all councillors automatically progress step by step 'down' each column in parallel, like well-trained Grenadiers. Nevertheless, there is evidence to show that orientations do cluster together at particular points in a councillor's career. Thus Newton found that the delegate role appealed particularly to the member for a marginal ward, whilst trustees were more likely to come from safe wards (Newton, 1974b, p.621). In Sunderland, and also in Glasgow, junior councillors, in their first term of office, were found to endorse a ward focus and adopt a watchdog role, with wider horizons developing later on (McKinsey & Co., 1973, p.35; Budge *et al.*, 1972, p.88). A tendency for junior members to prefer dealing with individual problems and for senior members to prefer general policy matters was found in Birmingham (Newton, 1974b, p.625). The tendency for junior councillors to spend some time 'finding their feet', before they are able to advance to specialist and then generalist policy making was noted in Barking and Kensington and Chelsea (Rees and Smith, 1964, p.42; Dearlove, 1973, pp.123-30) and Dearlove observed that the tradition that new councillors should 'sit down and shut up' might well turn their energies outwards from the council chamber to casework during their early years on the council. The same result may follow from the tradition whereby new members can rarely get the committee assignments they wish for: their long apprenticeship through minor committees may also turn their activities towards ward and constituent's problems. Junior councillors, freshly plucked from the local party branches, are also perhaps more likely to retain local contacts and ideological zeal before being subjected to later socialisation into the conventions and preoccupations of their more senior council colleagues. Moreover, their involvement in local ward issues may bring them into active contact with pressure groups outside the council, whereas senior councillors preoccupied with council work may have at best only honorific links with such groups. In terms of the links between the councillor's style and his relations with constituents and local party branches, Newton found that delegate councillors had most contact with branches and constituents, trustees least; delegates were also more willing to accept instructions on policy from local party branches than were politicos or trustees (Newton, 1974b, p.622).

The available evidence would seem to support the hypothesis that one can identify two internally consistent clusters of role orientations characterising junior and senior councillors. The two sets of attributes may for convenience's sake be described as those of the 'tribune' and the 'statesman' (cf., the 'country party' and 'Ministerialists' identified by Lee (1963)). Such a distinction certainly simplifies our discussion of the councillor's role and is borne out by current evidence. Like other classifications, however, it is not wholly watertight and individual councillors will not always fall into place within it. Some long-serving councillors in safe wards may enjoy the tribune role and never aspire to, or attain, the position of statesman. Conversely some councillors may possess talents which earmark them for immediate recruitment

into the statesman's rank, especially when there is a sudden turnover in
the membership of the council which depletes the ranks of the elder
statesmen. There is also evidence that party loyalty effects a councillor's
role to some degree. In Sheffield Labour councillors were more likely
to retain a belief in the importance of representing the interests of
individual ward members than were Conservatives (Hampton, 1970,
pp.196-7). As Heclo observed Labour wards are in any case likely to
generate individual and ward social problems (Heclo, 1969, p.200).
Indeed the safe Labour wards which provide most hope of secure
tenure to the statesman councillor on the Labour side may generate
sufficient casework to force a combination of policy and casework
activities even on a busy committee chairman. Longer services on the
Council may in itself lead to wider public recognition and hence to a
greater flow of individual casework. Heclo also makes the point that
casework may have different connotations for councillors of different
parties: on the Labour side it may mean advice bureaux and social
problems, on the Conservative side it may mean more general socialising
at fêtes, coffee mornings and the like (1969, p.191). Moreover it is
always possible for a councillor to encourage or discourage casework
by his own activity, or lack of it, in seeking out and dealing with
constituents' problems.

Aside from the impact of party allegiance on the councillor's role
there are other influences that may be significant. Clearly the fact of
being a member of a Majority Party may enable a councillor to acquire
policy making experience denied to a Minority councillor. Newton thus
suggests that Majority Group members are more likely to focus on the
level of city-wide concern rather than on ward representation (Newton,
1974b, p.623). Residence in the ward represented may make a
councillor more likely to identify with it and also more accessible to
those wishing to place problems before him. Finally an early entry to
the council in terms of age may enable a councillor to build up the
experience and seniority necessary to adopt the role of statesman: those
who are elected late in life may not get this opportunity.

The division between tribunes and statesmen is, at least theoretically,
one which exists at a given point in time, and is one which an individual
councillor can transcend during the course of a political career. However,
the increasing complexity of policy making may make the process of
graduation from one role to another more difficult. In the light of the
experience of corporate planning in one London Borough it is argued
that the consequences of this new form of decision making has been 'to
strengthen the split between those members who are interested in

policy and others who are interested in casework' (Cartwright, 1974, p.11). If this proves to be generally the case then it clearly has important implications for the ways in which local councils operate as a corporate body of councillors.

There remains one other aspect of the councillor's role, not considered in the discussion so far. This is the role of the councillor who serves on two councils within the two-tier structure. The key question here is whether the councillor concerned sees himself as having a two-way function – explaining each authority to the other and attempting to improve relations between them, in other words acting as a mediator, or as having a one-way function – acting as an ambassador for one of the authorities, trying to bring pressure to bear on its behalf. Dual membership is a subject on which we have little information. Prior to reorganisation it was argued that dual membership was 'the most important form of linkage between authorities' and that lower-tier authorities were so well represented on county committees that the main problem had proved to be 'one of finding ways of damping down the expressions of sectional interests' (CMLG, 1967, vol.2, table 1.39). Comprehensive figures for the new authorities are not available. However, in the metropolitan counties, where the old county borough traditions pose practical problems for the operation of a new two-tier system, the percentage of county councillors who are also district councillors is as follows: Greater Manchester 13, Merseyside 36, South Yorkshire 35, Tyne and Wear 20, West Midlands 59, and West Yorkshire 26. One reason for the wide variation is the variety of approaches adopted by the political parties which dominate the metropolitan counties. Neither of the two major parties attempted to impose any central policy on dual membership at the 1973 elections (Carlton and Dawson Interviews), and thus varying local strategies were adopted for, against or indifferent towards candidacies for two authorities. As far as the manner in which the dualist role develops it seems prima facie reasonable to suggest that much depends on how the councillor's career develops at county level. Once he becomes involved in issues of county-wide policy he may find it increasingly difficult to act as a mere ambassador for his own local district interests. He may then change from an ambassadorial to a mediatory interpretation of his dual role. As he approaches the rank of a statesman at County Hall he may find that the pressures are such that the simplest solution is to shed the dual role by resignation from the District Council.

The ability of the councillor to perform his role adequately has been a recurrent theme in the literature of local government, usually, however,

cast in terms of the councillor's intrinsic calibre rather than in terms of
defining the job and then assessing the human and material resources
necessary to perform it well. In the absence of any such definition it is
clearly impossible to be precise as to the qualities that might be
desirable in a councillor. Complaints about the calibre of councillors
are no new phenomenom, having been voiced in the middle and late
nineteenth century (Hennock, 1973, p.312; Jones, 1969, p.150). In the
course of time a variety of qualities have been identified. In the 1830s
the ideal councillor was seen as a man of station, of property and of
intelligence or education, whilst later in the century the specific
practical abilities of the businessman were cited (Hennock, 1973,
pp.308, 317). The notion of defining calibre in terms of social and
economic standing was repeated by Dame Evelyn Sharp in 1962 when
she argued that local government did not have enough people 'from
business, from industry, from agriculture, from the professions' (Sharp,
1962, p.383). If the real problem is one of lack of recruitment from
these sectors of society then it may be an insoluble problem. Clements
argues that those in senior positions in such fields find politics
distasteful to them since in its democratic and partisan form it 'is
resistant to the type of individual leadership, responsibility, decision-
making and receipt of deference to which most of (them) are
accustomed' and is liable to face them with 'a built in opposition
seeking to eject them from their positions and questioning the validity
of some at least of their fundamental premises' (Clements, 1969,
p.179, and p.185). This hesitancy towards being involved in the
hurly-burly of competitive politics was noted also by Lee who observed
that in Chester there was 'a tendency for business and professional
people not to submit themselves to election more than once, unless
they were Liberals' (Lee, in Sharpe, 1967, p.85).

In any event it is arguable that were such individuals to find their
way on to local councils this would only serve to make them even less
socially representative than they are at the moment. The desirable
skills for a councillor may not necessarily be a mere function of social
or economic status. This is the conclusion reached by Jones (1969,
p.158), by Harrison and Norton (CMLG, 1967, vol.5, p.41) and by
Sharpe (1962). Thus those qualities cited by Wiseman (1967, p.25)
may be found in all walks of life — an interest in detail, a capacity for
taking pains, hard-headedness and common sense: to this list might be
added those mentioned by D.M. Hill (1974, p.141) — bargaining ability,
critical judgement, and interpersonal skills.

The real problem may lie not in some mythical decline in the calibre

of councillors, for there is no evidence of a decline in the availability of
the skills cited by Wiseman and Hill. What may be occurring is that
'the increasing complexity of proposals for innovations are tending to
increase the gap in understanding between member and officer' (CMLG,
1967, vol.5, p.458). The practical issue is one of enabling the
councillors that we have to cope with the demands of the job they are
trying to do.

The Officers of the Council

Legally local government officers are the servants of the council which
appoints them: they are moreover servants of the council as a whole,
not of individual councillors or of a Majority Party. In their work their
activities are circumscribed by the policies laid down from time to
time by the council and its committees. Recruitment into the local
government service has traditionally been from the ranks of secondary
school leavers and from professionally qualified people. The tendency
for more and more professions to provide for graduate entry is likely to
lead in turn to more graduates entering local authority employment.
Appointment to local government posts is made nowadays on a merit
basis, although in the last century it was not unknown for them to be
made on political grounds (Hanham, 1959, p.396; Fraser, 1973, p.777).
In the present century the latter practice is, outwardly at least,
unknown, although its merits were still debated between the wars, when
George Lansbury argued in favour of Labour councils appointing
sympathetic officials, a notion dismissed by Herbert Morrison as one
that would encourage 'political servility and personal toadyism'
(Donoughue and Jones, 1973, p.53). As things are, given the variety of
political complexions encountered amongst the numerous local
authorities, it is always possible for an officer to seek work with one
whose political sympathies are attractive to him. Amongst councillors
the political views[2] — real or imagined — of officers are discussed on
occasion and, given the existence of informal contacts between members
of different authorities, it is always possible for soundings to be taken
as to the 'suitability' of officers for any posts which may be politically
sensitive. This is however an unexplored area, and given its delicacy, is
likely to remain so. All that can be said is that in England it is not the
case, as it is in West Germany, that senior local government officers are
likely to be active members of a political party, and in most cases it is
unlikely that they owe their appointment to being supporters of the
right party at the right place at the right time.

     For most senior officers a local government career involves

geographical moves as well as movement up the hierarchy. They are spiralists *par excellence.* Musgrove (1961, p.364) found that senior officers in Midland City[3] had moved about once every eight years since they were twenty-one years of age. Given the nature of local government employment it is natural that mobility should be a requirement for promotion since each authority has only one top job in any given field. Nevertheless it does permit the charge that if doctors bury their mistakes, local government officers can wave them goodbye as they entrain for their next job up the ladder.

This may perhaps seem a somewhat flippant view of the subject but it does emphasise the fact that local government officers are not necessarily all that local. Indeed by the time they achieve chief officer (or deputy chief officer) rank they have probably developed an outlook more cosmopolitan than local, and one which may well be more cosmopolitan than that of the councillors they serve. Through their activities in nationwide professional bodies, and local authority associations, through their contacts with fellow professionals in other walks of life, and through their dealings with Whitehall they may develop wider horizons, and different perspectives from local councillors. This may not be by any means a bad thing, but in one case at least it led one councillor to complain that 'too many chief officers are collaborating with ministerial departments without even notifying the elected civil heads' (Letter by Councillor J. Reddell, *Sunday Times,* 26 January 1969). It does seem probable that chief officers have greater opportunities for moving on a national stage than many councillors, restricted as the latter are both by shortage of time and by the lack of any arena other than the local authority associations.

Mention has been made of the role of professional bodies as a means for enabling officers to develop wider horizons and contacts than their purely local responsibilities would allow. This is but one aspect, however, of the significance of professionalism in the local government world. From its historic basis in the provision of certain public services with a high degree of technical import local government has developed around a number of professions, some of them indeed wholly or largely concentrated on local government itself, for example public health inspection, town and country planning, and weights and measures administration. Departments based on professional expertise have been the traditional structures within which officers have been employed. The administrators in local government have existed in order to service the professionals, rather than to interpret them as in central government. When the need arises to bring professional insights and recommendations before the politicians it is the professional officer who does so, not some local equivalent of the generalist Whitehall civil servant. If then local government is a stronghold of professionalism, it is nevertheless true that the stronghold is under some attack at the present time. The critiques of professionalism which are currently mounted in the local government context are three in number. They relate to the alleged failures of the professions concerned to relate satisfactorily to the local authority as a corporate body, to the councillors as politicians, and to their clients as citizens.

The first criticism is one which has been voiced by a number of commentators concerned with the management of local authorities. Thus the Maud Committee warned that 'professional exclusiveness undoubtedly militates against departmental co-ordination' (CMLG, 1967, vol.1, para.108). The managerial innovations proposed by the Maud Report had as one of their prime aims the overcoming of this professional exclusiveness in favour of a more integrated approach to policy making within the authority. The problem of professional isolationism is not, however, merely one of management structures. It derives also from the nature of professionalism. In particular it derives from the fact that professional officers, in carrying out their work, may have a sense of commitment to standards and values set by the professional bodies to which they belong and in whose traditions they have been educated. These professional standards may not always be in harmony: the utilitarian ethics of the highway engineer and the aesthetic values of the planner for example may provide the cause of some dispute on road lines and landscaping requirements. There are thus inevitable difficulties by virtue of the fact that different professions see the authority's problems − and their solution − in rather different lights and are likely to continue to do so as long as each profession adheres to its own traditional norms. Moreover the profession may not only be an officers' reference group in terms of standards and values: it may also be an important reference group in terms of career prospects. The likelihood of promotion to the most senior posts in local government can be enhanced by a good reputation in the professional world as well as by a good record with previous employers. The danger exists of an officer seeing a local problem as an admirable opportunity to display his own particular technical virtuosity and thereby make a name for himself in the profession. There is no reason to be surprised at the existence of professional exclusiveness and interdepartmental rivalry within an authority since it is inherent in the very nature of the professions, which are essentially exclusive bodies. The introduction of

managerial reforms may avoid the worst of the problem but is unlikely
to cure it entirely. All professions have their sticking point, and if they
want strongly to pursue individual lines they will do so. As J.G. Davies
observes 'it is not unknown. . .for officers to pursue their rivalry
through the medium of speeches made by politicians in the Council
chamber, with one department briefing one councillor and the rival
department briefing another' (Davies, J.G., 1972a, p.91).

The complaint that officers are not always able to relate satisfactorily
to the councillors as politicians arises from the fact that the two sets of
people approach the problem of decision making in rather different
ways. To those schooled in a profession, especially one with a fairly
high technical content, it is hard to admit that a proposal which is
apparently right on technical grounds can be dismissed on 'mere'
political grounds. The notion that there are objectively correct solutions
to problems lies at the heart of much professional education. Moreover,
'the development of expertise usually generates a sense of dedication,
and it is understandable that many bureaucrats identify this dedication
with the public interest' (William Niskanen Jr., in Nicholson & Topham,
1972, p.27). Thus it is all too easy for professional officers to believe
that their own views are both correct and in the public interest, and that
they are moreover self-evidently so. Unfortunately experts, of any sort,
are always liable to exaggerate the importance of their own specialism,
and to lose sight of wider perspectives. The type of problem that then
arises is illustrated by Elkin in regard to open space plans for the
World's End area of Chelsea when 'the terms of the discussion. . .were
set by professional values concerning acceptable standards rather than
"political" considerations of what might be acceptable to various groups
of concerned citizens' (Elkin, 1974a, p.75). In recent years however the
notion that 'professional values concerning acceptable standards' have
some unquestioned merit has become less acceptable to many politicians.
The consequences of high-rise flats, of urban motorways, and of town
centre redevelopment schemes for example have caused many laymen
to wonder whether architects, engineers and planners really knew what
they were doing, and whether their standards were really relevant to the
lives they ultimately affected. Similarly, in the saga of the Third London
Airport, the successive insistences of various experts that the only
possible site was at Stansted, then Wing, then Foulness served to suggest
firstly that experts could not always agree on a right answer and
secondly that they were as likely to be wrong as to be right.

Councillors, as politicians, have their own 'professional' standards
and values, based variously upon ideology, party loyalty, identification

with particular interests and groups, and political self-preservation and advancement. These standards and values, except in the case of the most rigid of politicians, cohabit in mixtures that vary from time to time and from issue to issue. Professional officers brought up in a tradition of supposedly value-free technical objectivity may understandably find it hard to cope with attitudes which seem to them to consist of special pleading, of party in-fighting or of jockeying for position. Similarly, doubts amongst the politicians as to the reliability of expert advice can only serve to widen rather than bridge the gap between the two groups.

It is tempting to wonder whether the problems outlined above, of professional exclusiveness and of the gap between the professional officer and the politician might not be ameliorated by the development of some equivalent of the generalist Civil Servant able to match and blend expert advice from different quarters, to present it to the politicians in forms more suited to their preoccupations, and free from any single departmental loyalties. However, even if such an innovation proved both possible and successful it is doubtful whether it would deal with the third criticism of professionalism in local government, that relating to client relationships.

Two essential features of professions have been their possession of criteria as to what constituted good practice and the willingness of clients to accept those criteria and thus to accept the professional's solutions. These features seem to be somewhat eroded amongst the newer local government professions, most notably those which deal directly with urban social problems, the town planners and the social workers. Although it originated in the early years of the century the planning profession has enjoyed its main period of growth in the years since the Second World War, and during this time its character changed as incoming social scientists began to outnumber architects, engineers and surveyors (Cockburn, 1970, pp.22-4). Social work, despite its long history, has been slow to develop a single professionalism although its component parts have developed their own specialist education and organisations, for health visitors, child care officers, education welfare officers, etc.

Both in regard to town planning and to social work there has emerged a body of criticism as to the right and the ability of practitioners to tell their clients what is the right solution to their problem, especially when the practitioners are operating through traditional local bureaucracies. In the case of planning the problem of identifying the nature of good practice has been highlighted by the emergence of a dispute as to what the aims of the profession should be.

There has emerged in England a division of opinion already noted in the
United States where 'the profession is being split into progressive and
conservative wings, the former calling for social planning to reduce
economic and racial inequality, the latter defending traditional physical
planning and the legitimacy of middle-class values' (Gans, 1972, p.91;
see also Palmer, 1972, for a similar British view). For some planners the
traditional assumptions of their profession and of their local authority
employers have proved too narrow or insensitive, leading to the emergence
of the 'bureaucratic guerilla' who works for the council during the day,
and against it, on behalf of local residents, out of office hours (Eversley,
1973, p.219). It is not only within the profession that doubts have arisen.
Two writers, both local politicians as well as academics, have attacked what
they see as an excess of arrogance and professional presumption amongst
planners (Davies, J.G., 1972a; Dennis, 1972a). In the meantime, the
profession has continued to be locked in a seemingly interminable debate as to
what its true character and role should be (for example McLoughlin, 1973).

    In social work the question of relations with the client have been
well to the fore of the debate. There has been recognition that the
client may have a totally different perspective on his situation from that
of the professional social worker (Mayer and Timms, 1970). One
consequence has been that 'a growing body of critics of professionalisation
in social work. . .see the process of professionalisation as tending
to increase the social distance between social workers and
clients, deflecting social workers from social change agent roles, and
generally inducing social workers to adhere to the status quo' (Leonard,
1973, p.115). By the more radical social workers 'the client is now
assumed to be able to make some judgement of his own needs' instead
of languishing in comparative ignorance (Leonard, op.cit., pp.113-4).
The traditional role of the local authority social worker as a 'social
lubricant' rather than a 'social catalyst' (Brill, 1971), is thus called into
question with the result that 'the image of the social worker as expert
therapist is today being replaced by the image of the radical community
worker' whose client 'is no longer the sick person but the sick society'
(Rankin, 1971, pp.20-1). This new attitude may owe something to the
recruitment into recently expanded Social Service Departments of
workers whose previous experience has been with voluntary
organisations with radical aspirations such as Shelter. Such an attitude
clearly runs counter to traditional local authority professional practice
and it has on occasion led to direct clashes between radical social
workers and their employing authorities.[4]

    Amongst the more radical planners and social workers a unifying theme is that the 'slogan for all (client) groups is "don't call me, I'll call you"' (Hang and Sussman, 1969, p.156). This belief, together with a specific commitment to egalitarian aims rather than pretensions to value-free objectivity, characterises both groups of anti-professionals. Their common ground has led some to see in them the seeds of new forms of social and community planning which would not be rooted in professional bureaucracies or the formal politics of the council chamber (Palmer, 1973). Clearly the whole development of this school of thought can be related to the growth of community action as a form of social action and social provision outside, and sometimes in opposition to, the statutory processes of local government.

Councillors and Officers: the Relationships

The local government officer is the servant of the council as a corporate body, not of any single committee or chairman or member. Thus whereas the Whitehall civil servant has one political master — the Minister — the local government officer has in a sense, many masters, in that there is no single fount of authority other than the body of councillors assembled and voting. Moreover, in the process of deliberation that leads up to that voting the officer can be called on for advice and information by any individual member of the council, each of whom has equal rights of access to that officer. Moreover, each Chief Officer has equal access to any councillor and vice versa, regardless of that councillor's membership of a particular party group or a particular committee of the authority.

The consequence of this is of course that local government officers, of senior rank at least, are far more likely to be in frequent contact with councillors than are civil servants with members of parliament (who are not, after all, their employers). The fact that so much of the work of the council is done by committees clearly brings officers and members into close working contact. But it should not be thought that this is the only mechanism by which the two groups interact. In addition to formal meetings of the council and its committees there are working groups of members and officers, agenda conferences, site visits and tours of inspection, trips to conferences, meetings with other councils and with central government, public meetings, and functions such as receptions and ceremonial openings. At such occasions members and officers will be meeting together under conditions of varying formality and informality. These events can be, intentionally or otherwise, useful mechanisms for resolving problems, sounding out opinions, lobbying support and floating ideas.[5] Beyond this there are the personal contacts between individual members and officers, from appointments on specific problems, through 'button-holing in the corridor', to the chance encounter and the telephone conversation all of which provide similar opportunities for the exploration of ideas and the exercise of influence. In some cases there may even be out-of-hours contacts in which, even if official business is not discussed, mutual respect and sympathies may be developed.[6]

The whole issue of member-officer contacts outside formal meetings of the council and its committees is largely unexplored at present. If it is true that 'the more frequently men interact with one another, the more alike they become in the norms they hold' (Homans, 1951, p.126) the nature and frequency of such contacts is clearly a legitimate area of concern for those interested in the inner workings of local authorities.

Within the area of formal meetings of the council and its committees the member-officer relationship is, on paper, clear. The officers are present to advise and to recommend, but the members must make the final decisions. Few officers would commit themselves openly to the blunt view of Sir Arthur Binns, that councillors 'should be led to the right conclusions under the impression that they are arriving at it under their own steam' (quoted in Kogan, 1973, p.48). Even fewer, one imagines, would take it upon themselves to say, as did Joseph Heron, Town Clerk of Manchester, 'Councillor X, you know nothing about the matter. Please sit down.' (Simon, 1938, p.408.) In Dearlove's phrase, it is virtually 'impossible to break through the cultural cliché that they (the officers) were simply servants advising the all-powerful policy making councillors whose decisions they readily implemented' (Dearlove, 1973, p.229). Yet this 'cultural cliche' of local government obscures the reality, which can be rather different.

The reality of the formal proceedings of council and committee meetings is that the elected members meet in the presence of officers to consider reports prepared by the officers containing recommendations for action made by the officers. The meetings thus differ from other meetings of public laymen such as MPs, Cabinet Ministers or jurymen, in that information and advice from experts is rendered in person whilst the process of decision making is under way. This at the very least offers to the officers the opportunity for the well-timed remark, the cautionary aside to the chairman, even the occasional sigh or grimace, which might prevent the councillors taking a decision unwelcome to the officers. Moreover the attendance of officers at meetings is not governed by the same rules as those applying to councillors' membership of committees. Thus it is always open for any number of chief officers to attend and, if they wish to, present a united front of expertise whose very size may sway the wavering member.[7] Of course the contributions which officers make in the meetings of a council or its committee will depend greatly on the chairman. In some authorities no officers at all will speak at full council meetings – other than the Clerk perhaps on some procedural issue – leaving the various committee chairmen to speak for their committees. In the committee meetings officers will of course speak when called upon to do so, but some will seek to intervene on their own initiative if the chairman will allow it. The extent to which a chairman is in awe of his officers will clearly have an impact in this situation.

Aside from the ability of officers to be present at meetings, in varying strength, and to participate in the debate, another factor of some consequence is that the discussion must focus around the documents presented to the members. It seems reasonable to assume that this places some advantage with those who prepare the documents and who are familiar with the wider body of information on which they are based. The information collected by a local authority is gathered primarily for the use of officers, rather than members, and reaches members only after a filtering process which may dilute and occasionally distort its nature. Members must thus take on trust the contents of the documents which comprise the agenda before them at a meeting, and must rely for further elaboration on the verbal exposition that an officer may choose to give. Dennis (1972b) has argued that this situation is open to three possible abuses. An officer may overestimate his own knowledge and underestimate his own interest in how an issue is resolved: he may substitute his professional standing for weight of evidence and rely on it to outface any amateur doubts of a member: and he may come to have an interest in preserving the notion that previous information and policies were correct even though experience has called them into question. Such problems of distortion, omission or misrepresentation are much more likely to be a matter of innocent and unconscious bias, and perhaps of occasional professional self-preservation, than of bad faith or conscious malpractice on the part of officers. They stem from the fact that the control of information and its presentation is very largely in the hands of the officers, and that the members have to take what they are given. 'In Coventry we were able to see much evidence of the powerful position which a chief officer could achieve through his control over the flow of information' (Friend and Jessop, 1969, p.55).

In addition to controlling the flow of information and of

recommendations the officers may also be able to participate in the actual process of decision taking by suggesting the appropriate wording of resolutions or amendments and of course by being responsible for drafting the minutes of the meeting.

The extent to which officers are allowed to make the running in the way suggested above will depend of course on the willingness of the members, and especially committee chairmen, to let them. The business of the authority must be carried on, and if members are happy not to ask too many awkward questions, the officers can hardly be blamed for getting on with the job in hand as expeditiously as possible according to their lights. There is little information as to what predisposes councillors to scrutinise the officers' work with special care. Sharpe has suggested that party may be a factor here in that Labour seems 'to keep a tighter rein on its officers than the Conservatives' (Sharpe, 1973, p.25). It may be the case that similar social backgrounds enable Conservative councillors and their officers to share an easy relationship based on similar assumptions about policy and its implementation. Labour councillors in contrast may suspect middle-class officers of secret leanings to the Right and may thus be more liable to check up that they are following the policies laid down by a Labour majority.

The councillor-officer relationship is not an easy one at the best of times. The councillor brings to it his political skill and his legitimation through election along with his legal responsibilities as final decision maker. The officer possesses resources of access to information, professional expertise, and a full-time commitment. Whether this makes for equality in partnership as local government becomes more complex is doubtful. Harrison and Norton observed that 'most officers seemed of the opinion that only a minority of members on their committees made any real contribution' and in their own view 'cases of clear purposeful discussion with a good level of understanding and contribution from all the participants were rare' (CMLG, 1967, vol.5, pp.42 and 43). In private conversation it is notable that councillors will often admit to the great power of officers *vis-à-vis* the members even to the point of wondering who is supposed to be in charge. The equivalent admission is rarely made by serving Cabinet Ministers. This may be because the collective responsibility of a committee is more diffused than the individual responsibility of a Minister, and hence a councillor's admission of weakness before local officials is to confess a corporate rather than a personal failing.

Policy and its Execution

There is another problem in the field of member-officer relations in addition to those already noted. This concerns their respective roles within the authority in terms of making and carrying out policy.

Concern over this issue implies that there is perhaps some correct division of labour between the job of the member and the job of the officer, and that such a demarcation is essential to the proper conduct of local government. Such a notion has little basis in law, in that formally the councillors are as much responsible for deciding matters of detail as they are for deciding on broad issues of policy. Historically, too, members' interests in details as well as policy is no new phenomenom but goes back to the middle of the last century when there was lacking any reliable body of professionally qualified experts to whom the work could be safely entrusted (Hennock, 1973, p.8). An examination of local government decision making will show that in practice both officers and members can expect to be involved at a variety of stages in the process.

The formal process of decision making in a local authority may be represented by the following stages:[8]

1. Chief Officer identifies a new problem or an opportunity.
2. Chief Officer makes recommendations to committee.
3. The committee makes a decision.
4. The council endorses the decision.
5. The departmental officers implement the decision.

In practice, however, there are other stages involved which may not have any formal recognition in the council's procedures but are clearly of significance in reality. Thus for example before stage 1 is reached somebody — member or officer — must bring the new problem or opportunity to the notice of the chief officer. Before stage 2 is reached it may be necessary to consult with the committee chairman or with other senior councillors and with other chief officers before any recommendation goes to committee. Stages 3 and 4 can each be preceeded by party group meetings at which the effective decisions may in practice be taken and by officers' meetings to decide on the officers' 'line' at committee or at council. Finally, before stage 5 can commence officers must meet to decide how best to carry out the decisions of the councillors and they may wish to consult with the latter about this.

Thus at each stage in the process of decision making it is possible for both members and officers to be involved in their respective ways in everything from policy formulation to execution.

From the member's point of view this makes sense in so far as he has a political objective and wishes to ensure that it is not lost sight of at any stage from policy formulation to execution. Since the councillor is a political animal the key criteria by which to judge the propriety of his involvement is that of whether a particular issue — be it of policy or execution — has or may have political connotations. Similarly from the officer's standpoint there may be questions of financial practicality, of legal requirements, and of technical possibility which require airing at any of the various stages in the process.

The officer's task, after all is not merely to execute but to advise and advice can be appropriate at many levels of policymaking and implementation.

Much of the discussion which surrounds the issue stems from the fear that in fact members may, through choice or necessity, overinvolve themselves in execution, thereby leaving policy formulation to the officers. The resulting situation is the one described by Jones in Wolverhampton where policy 'was thought up by the officials who then planted the policy inside the minds of the Chairmen, who in their turn guided the committees' (Jones, 1969, p.177). A similar situation was said to exist at one time in the LCC where 'The officers were the active types. . .The officers were there to put forward suggestions, the members were there to see that the public would accept these suggestions.' (Elkin, 1974a, p.117.) It is thus no great surprise that Harrison and Norton noted that 'in nearly two-thirds of the local authorities we consulted, officers were said to make a significant contribution to the initiation of policy and in nearly a quarter they were said to play the major part'. This high degree of officer initiative in policy questions could be especially present when a council lacked any clear party majority, or when an issue presented no clear party line, or when the need to define a policy arose as a result of some central government directive received initially by departmental officers rather than by committee members (CMLG, 1967, vol.5, p.196).

Along with a high degree of officer initiative in policy making there has also been observed a high degree of member involvement in the details of policy execution, in some cases to a degree that causes concern to officers who find the practice inhibiting and prone to inefficiency. The reasons for members' preoccupation with detail may vary from an uneasiness at handling broad policy, to a distrust of the officers, or to a belief in their own role as a watchdog (CMLG, 1967, vol.5, pp.280-4). In small authorities of course there may always be the problem that

there just aren't enough major policy issues to keep the members
occupied anyway.

In an attempt to resolve the problems of what should be the proper
roles of members and officers in this context the Bains Committee
commended the notion of a continuum between policy at one end and
execution at the other with members predominating at the former and
officers at the latter (Department of the Environment, 1972b, p.11).
The ideas of continuum and of predominance rather than of demarcation
and exclusivity of roles is perhaps an improvement on more simplistic
schemes. More realistic yet, however, may be the notion that the
predominance at either end is not a matter of members or officers but
of senior members and senior officers at one end and of junior members
and junior officers at the other end. This formula may be as close an
approximation to reality as can be hoped for.

In practical terms the problems that come within the orbit of local
government require the bringing to bear of both professional expertise
and political values. Either of these may have something significant to
say about both ends and means. The exact methods of blending
expertise and values will vary from problem to problem and from place
to place. The key issue — if values are to prevail over expertise — is that
whatever the arrangements, the elected members should be able to secure
whatever method of matching expertise with values they consider
desirable in any given case. This may of course lead to a confused and
'fudged' picture to the outsider. However, it must be remembered that
both officers and members are seeking not some recondite truth of
administrative science but a comfortable and utilitarian working
arrangement which fits their particular requirements. The emphasis
thus falls on the working out of some locally acceptable practice rather
than any universally applicable prescription. Once that has been done
then the questions for the observer become how was the practice
arrived at, is it ever challenged, by whom, under what circumstances, on
what grounds, with what results? In particular, the key question becomes
who has the last word on those issues that — rightly or wrongly — the
politicians regard as being of political consequence?

The Institutions of the Council

So far our discussion of what takes place within the local authority has
concentrated on the individuals concerned — the members and the
officers — and their relationships rather than on the formal structures
or institutions of the council. Nevertheless, something must be said of
these, since their character and procedings are integral to the way in

which a local authority deals with its business.

With the growth in the workload of local authorities it became more and more the case that the committees were the key points in the formal structure of decision making, with the full council serving merely to endorse all but those most important of matters reserved to it. Consequently, the full meeting of the council became less and less a place where issues are debated prior to a decision being made. Like the House of Commons the council meeting, held perhaps only once every six weeks or even less frequently, has become essentially a platform for informing the public of intended policies, for establishing party positions and scoring party points, for enhancing (or diminishing) the reputation of individual politicians, and for the public presentation of individual or sectional interests or grievances. At such meetings individual councillors may establish their reputation as fiery speakers, as skilled debators or as masters of procedure, and party groups may exhibit their solidarity and the diligence of their whips, but unless there is a very uncertain political balance on the council it is unlikely that major political upsets will take place. In effect the council meeting has become the 'theatre' of local government, where set-piece confrontations can take place and where heroes and villains can be identified before the audience of press and public gallery.

The 'workshop' of local government is the committee meeting wherein the bulk of the formal business of the authority is transacted. The Webbs trace the origins of local administration by committee back into the eighteenth century. In the parishes vestry committees ran the workhouses and checked the parish accounts; in the counties committees of quarter sessions dealt with public nuisances, vagrancy, prisons and repair of bridges (Webb, S and B, 1963, pp.130-2 and 529-33). With the evolution of modern local government in the nineteenth century the role of committees came to be one of making recommendations to the full council and then following up the decision of the council to ensure that it was properly implemented. The increasing burden of local authority responsibilities and the unwieldy nature of the full council as a forum of discussion have led to more and more powers being delegated to committees, and indeed to chairmen and officers as well. Any of the council's functions, other than the levying of the rate or borrowing money, may be delegated to its committees and there has thus been a wide variation in both the extent of delegation and the items chosen to be delegated (Greenwood *et al.*, 1969).

The practice of relying on committees to deal with the bulk of the authority's business means that the committees have in a sense attempted a return to the role of their eighteenth-century forbears, directly concerned with administering particular services rather than with merely preparing recommendations for the full council. It is, however, questionable how far committees can really administer effectively. Although Wheare (1955, ch.7) specifically categorises local government committees as 'committees to administer' it was the conclusion of Harrison and Norton that 'the typical local government committee, because of its cumbersome nature and its discontinuity, cannot administer in the normal sense of the word' (CMLG, 1967, vol.5, p.496). The need to overcome problems of discontinuity and of cumbersomeness, has led increasingly to the setting up of sub-committees, working groups and panels of members and to delegation to chairmen and to officers. In practice what has happened over the years is that it has been recognised that the full council, and then later the full committee, is unable to bring all its members together sufficiently frequently, and that even when it does so the instrument of administration thus created is unwieldy. Consequently, the search has been for smaller structures, more frequently in session, from sub-committees through the whole range of committee substitutes to the full-time officer and, in some larger authorities, the virtually full-time chairman.

There are of course some things which a committee can do, and do well. It is an admirable institution for collective thinking aloud, for bargaining and conciliation, for educating members and officers in each other's ways and for enabling complaints and problems to be aired. But of itself a committee is unlikely to generate new ideas, though it may adopt those produced elsewhere, and it is dependent on particular individuals, notably officers, for the paperwork on which it feeds and for the correct drafting of any paperwork which it does itself produce or cause to be produced. These characteristics were among those which led the Maud Committee to argue that in future committees should cease to have any pretensions towards executive or administrative roles and should become mainly deliberative bodies (CMLG, 1967, vol.1, para.8). In practice the forms of deliberation thus envisaged would have been those concerned with investigation and exhortation in relation to past, present and future performance (ibid., para.166). One consequence of this role for the local authority committee would have been that the committee chairman would have ceased to have any significant function other than that of chairing meetings. Moreover, the members of the proposed managing body, the management board, would not have inherited any individual accountability for the running of particular

services (ibid., paras.210 and 211). In retrospect it is clear that this line
of development ran counter to what was in practice finding favour in
local authorities. There would no longer have been any political figure
in the council with responsibility for any individual service, and thus no
single figure to whom inquiries, entreaties or accusations could be
addressed whether by fellow politicians, officers, electors or the media.
Nor would there have been any individual political figure with sufficient
commitment to a single service to encourage him to develop ideas, draft
proposals and lobby for support in the way that a committee itself –
deliberative or executive – could never do. In short, the proposals of
the Maud Committee for dealing with the shortcomings of the
traditional committee failed to take account of the need for clear
political accountability in each area of the council's work. In doing so
they seemingly ignored the very relevant comments of Harrison and
Norton (CMLG, 1967, vol.5, para.172):

> . . .it appears likely that many of the influences and needs which
> have resulted in the accretion of functions to the office of committee
> chairman will continue to operate in the same way. In particular, it
> may be expected that the political responsibility for a service will
> more and more clearly devolve upon the chairman. . .it may well be
> felt that this should be formally recognised by an open definition of
> the committee chairman's role. . .(which) would make the office
> more challenging, more obviously demanding of ability and initiative,
> and would help to make the system in general more comprehensible
> to the public.

In legal terms, at present chairmen of local authority committees have
no more power than their 'backbench' colleagues, other than that of
controlling the conduct of meetings, unless specific powers are delegated
to them by members. The extent of their influence over officers is likely
to be very much a question of personal qualities. Legally again, the
officers are no more beholden to a chairman than to any other single
councillor, but of necessity the relationship is rather different from the
normal councillor-officer relationship. At the turn of the century, when
officers were not as fully professional as today, and when some were
still only employed part-time, it was possible for a long-serving chairman
to be the effective equal of his chief officer especially when possessed
of a superior social status as well (cf. Jones, 1969, pp.229-41). Today a
chairman is rarely likely to be the superior of an officer either in
professional or in social standing and if he seeks an ascendancy it must

be based on personal or political factors or both. In particular much may depend on how a chairman has attained the chair. The actual process of selection may be by vote of the committee members, or of the full council, or of a special selection committee; or effectively, by nomination of the Majority Group or its leader. Where the chairmanship comes as a reward for mastery of a particular field of operations or as a recognition of political skills then there is some hope that chairman and chief officer may deal on equal terms. When the chairmanship is a mere recognition of seniority there is a danger that it may bring the weariness, rather than the wisdom, of years.

Handling the chairman-chief officer relationship is not of course the sole content of the chairman's role. Arguably, however, it is a key to successfully blending the political and professional components of local authority business. The chairman certainly has other duties, notably as spokesman for his committee to other committees, to the Majority Group, to the council, to central government and to the community at large. Yet his ability to do any of these effectively depends on the ability to present a united front of chairman and chief officer so that any attacks may be repelled from whatever quarter they may come. There is of course always the danger that in seeking such security in his necessarily exposed position, the chairman will deliver himself wholly into the hands of his chief officer, whose mouthpiece he then becomes. This merely serves to emphasise the fact that in order to do his job properly the chairman must command those resources of personality, political skill, knowledge, understanding and time which will allow him to operate as an equal partner with his professional opposite number.

Concern over the ability of councils, committees and individual councillors to do their jobs properly found expression in the 1960s in a growing concern for institutional reform in local government. This was in part perhaps merely one aspect of a wider concern for institutional reform in British society as a whole during this period. In addition, people were realising that individual local social problems were often closely tied together, for example the close links between the child's home conditions and his school performance or between traffic levels and local environmental quality. The concern focused itself on two related issues: the problem of achieving co-ordination and even integration of hitherto separate local authority activities, and the need to concentrate councillor's energies into taking central policy initiatives instead of allowing them to be dissipated into a pre-occupation with questions of detail. The proposals of the Maud Committee saw the solution in a threefold division of labour with the officers dealing with administrative detail, the majority of councillors dealing with representation and deliberation, and a minority of councillors on a management board to take the initiative in overall supervision and in policy formulation.

These particular proposals were not universally popular, notably because of their tendency to detract from the collective responsibility of councillors and to divide them into 'first-class' and 'second-class' members (Greenwood *et al.,* 1969). The response of local government was on the whole not to set up Maud-style management boards but to establish co-ordinating policy committees under a variety of titles, most with powers of co-ordination, some with powers of initiative (Greenwood, Stewart and Smith, 1972).

The complete reorganisation of local government outside Greater London in the early 1970s gave an opportunity for the internal restructuring of management practices which the pre-existing authorities had somewhat shied away from (Lucking *et al.,* 1974). To guide the new authorities in this restructuring the Bains and Paterson reports recommended a number of innovations aimed at stressing a corporate rather than a departmental approach to local government. The reports' specific proposals included the setting up of a central policy and resources committee, and the establishment of a committee structure based on programme areas rather than on a one-department-one-committee link. There should be review and monitoring of performance by the policy and resources committee (Paterson), or by a sub-committee thereof (Bains), and the appointment of a chief executive free of departmental responsibilities and supported by a management team of principal chief officers (Department of Environment, 1972b; Scottish Development Department, 1973).

In the structures which were proposed for the new authorities and in those which were eventually adopted there emerged a trend towards implementation of the corporate philosophy at least on paper. This was especially the case in the English metropolitan authorities where there was almost universal adoption of a central policy committee. Virtually all the metropolitan authorities appointed a chief officer with corporate as well as, or instead of, purely departmental responsibilities, together with a management team of chief officers. In addition there was a general move towards the establishment of programme area committees, albeit not always the specific programme areas identified in the Bains Report. Outside the English metropolitan areas similar trends are visible. The main departure from the Bains' recommendations seems to lie in a wariness about establishing sub-committees of the policy and resources committee including one for performance review. One significant alignment with Bains occurs in the tendency to open the policy and resources committee to Minority Party members. This is something of a reversal of the practice that developed in the interval between the Maud and the Bains reports (Norton and Stewart, 1973; Greenwood *et al.,* 1974; Hinings *et al.,* 1974; Keast, 1974). In Scotland the Paterson Report made no recommendation on the party composition of the policy and resources committee, and the Labour-dominated council for the most populous region — Strathclyde — opted for a one party committee.

The move towards a more corporate form of policy making entailed in these new structures must assume that the local authority can evolve some corporate goals over and above traditional departmental goals of providing particular services. In practice, there are two possible sources from which these goals may be obtained, namely the collective deliberations of the officers and of the elected members. A major question which thus arises is whether councillors can use the new procedures of corporate planning effectively. Stewart has identified some of the components of corporate planning as being the identification of explicit objectives, explicit policy making, systematic policy review, increased need for policy analysis, and an increasing concern for the results of interaction between the local authority and its environment (Stewart, 1973a, pp.24-5). If members are to handle these aspects of corporate planning then they will need more resources than they have traditionally enjoyed. They will need the direct support and services of the new units for budgeting and research and intelligence. To absorb the output of information and advice they will need extra time. The sort of facilities which councillors will increasingly come to require have been summed up in proposals put forward during the 1973 County Elections in the manifesto of the Nottinghamshire Labour Party *The Way Ahead* (p.17):

We shall set up a proper members' secretariat to provide councillors with background information, statistics, previous committee decisions, information from other councils and government departments, etc., both on request and on the initiative of the department itself. It will be part of the council's Executive Office, but it must have close links with the council's research unit. One of its purposes, like that of the House of Commons library, will be to provide members with the means and material to assess independently the progress and work of the service departments. It should be the

normal channel for members' questions to departments: a large part
of a councillor's work is finding out information and getting fuller
explanations for members of the public, and this secretariat will take
away much of the burden, and make sure members of the public get
prompt answers. The section will also provide proper secretarial
services to members.

On winning control the Labour Group in Nottinghamshire began to
implement these proposals. For example, members' services were to
include a specialist library, information and research service which,
amongst other things, could circulate summaries of recent developments
in local government, prepare abstracts of journals and other literature,
assist members with enquiries made on behalf of electors, and carry out
small research projects on behalf of members. Associated with the
library would be a secretarial service for members. Provision was made
for committee chairmen and the Minority Group to have special
secretarial assistance and personal assistant staff.

Convinced that taking control requires 'being on the job', provision
was made for payment of allowances to each of the chairmen, Majority
and Minority Group officers and certain 'shadow' chairmen on any
'Duty Day' spent at County Hall 'in connection with the business of the
Council or his customary duties as a councillor'. This has enabled the
leading councillors on both sides to devote as much time as required to
the job to which they were elected. The key committee chairmen have in
effect become full-time professional councillors.

Nottinghamshire have not been alone in pioneering the provision of
resources that enable councillors to do their job. Members' information
rooms have been set up for example at Hammersmith, Havering and
Hull, members' libraries at Bristol and Liverpool. At the GLC services
to members include a Daily Intelligence Bulletin, a press cutting service,
a Members Information Officer, and a series of literature reviews under
the title *London Topics.*

The GLC also provide a members' secretariat to assist all members
with enquiries, correspondence, and keeping of papers on constituency
and council — but not party — business.

Among the more controversial schemes for aiding members has been
the appointment of personal assistants to senior councillors. Here the
GLC are in the vanguard following the commitment made to provide
'specialist help for committee chairmen' in the Labour manifesto *A
Socialist Strategy for London.* The arrangements now agreed and
operating at the GLC include not only a members' secretariat but

specific provision for personal assistants, as outlined below.

1. For the Leader of the Council, a Head and Deputy Head of his Private Office, an Executive officer, and two secretaries.
2. For the Leader of the Opposition, a personal assistant plus a secretary.
3. For chairmen on the GLC and ILEA, a total of fifteen personal assistants plus six secretaries.
4. For Opposition spokesmen, four personal assistants and two secretaries.

Prior to the introduction of the Personal Assistant scheme, the only facilities of this sort in existence at the GLC were the provision of an administrative assistant for the Leader of the Council plus a small group of secretarial staff: in addition, his party provided a political secretariat for dealing with party political matters. Under the new scheme the Leader's private office was reconstituted, with the head of the office being appointed from outside the council's service on a contract basis. The first head of the private office of Sir Reg Goodwin, Labour Leader of the GLC, was Peter Walker, a former employee of the Greater London Labour Party and a Croydon Borough councillor. The party political secretariat continued to be staffed by party employees. To enable both the head and deputy head of the Leader's private office to attend party group meetings a special suspension was agreed of a GLC standing order which would otherwise have prevented them doing so.

The allocation of personal assistants between the various committee chairman was handled by the Majority Party Chief Whip and has provided one assistant for each major committee chairman, with minor committee chairmen sharing the remainder. The tasks undertaken by the assistants vary according to the requirements of their chairmen, with some of the latter treating them as little more than filing clerks at first. However, the range of their work now includes liaison between chairmen and committee clerks, managing the chairman's diary and appointments, processing constituency business, filtering paperwork, gathering information and, when suitably briefed, acting as 'his master's voice'.

On the opposition side, the Minority Party's requirements are somewhat different, and the current Minority Leader sees the essential role of the assistants as being to help the Opposition to 'look for the chances' of tripping up the Majority Party, or of getting a majority proposal modified or of doing a mutually satisfactory deal on a delicate issue (Cutler interview).

As for the personal assistants themselves, they were all appointed from within the service of the GLC, mainly from younger members of the administrative staff. Their tenure is intended to be for a short-term period — perhaps two or three years — before they return to their normal duties with the council.

Clearly there are problems about how far these assistants can be or should be politicised. With the exception of the Head and Deputy Head of the Leader's Private Office, GLC Standing Orders prevent them from attending Party Group meetings. The extent to which they are kept politically 'in the know' depends very much on the predeliction of the member to whom they are assigned. However, although they are formally debarred from political contact, one of the qualities looked for when the appointments were made was evidence of political sensitivity.

It is probably too early to judge the full success or otherwise of this scheme. There is certainly a demand from within the ranks of GLC chairmen for more assistants to be made available. One problem may prove to be the reluctance of the assistants to return to more mundane duties after two or three years at the centre of the council's operations. In terms of working relations with other staff, the initial teething troubles have been cured but inevitably there remain certain problems associated with being simultaneously both a junior member of the staff and an emissary to senior staff on behalf of a committee chairman. At all events there are certainly no political pressures within the GLC to discontinue the scheme and it seems almost bound to survive any change in the balance of political power at County Hall.

Innovations such as those outlined above will doubtless assist individual councillors to function more effectively. Equally desirable are methods of ensuring that the process of policy making and implementation remains accountable to the councillors as a whole. In the present context of local government operations there are two major problems here. One concerns political control over performance, the other concerns political control over policy formulation.

No matter how integrated and corporate the philosophy and practice of a local authority may be, in carrying out its policies it is dependent on the performance of individual departments and their professional staff. If the councillors wish to have some influence in the way a policy is implemented — even if only by way of review, or by way of complaint over a particular instance — some mechanism of direct accountability is desirable. For all its faults the traditional arrangement of one committee — one department, with its associated chairman and chief officer relationship, did provide a direct avenue for bringing to bear political pressure on a particular department. It also of course provided departments with political allies in the form of chairmen and committee members who could argue a departmental case inside party groups. Severing the direct department-committee association sunders this link without effectively replacing it. The programme area committees — assuming they are more than just the old system under another name — make a group of departments responsible to the traditional collectivity of councillors. They make it more difficult to answer the question 'who is to blame?' (or 'who is to take the blame?') in an unequivocal fashion. It is conceivable that the need for an answer to that question will be found increasingly by making committee chairmen themselves more and more directly responsible politically for departmental performance within their programme area, a development which in the larger authorities at least, seems certain to herald the arrival of the full-time chairman.

Political control over policy formulation, rather than over performance, depends upon the existence of a political centre of initiative within the local authority. Here we must consider the ability of councillors to provide such a central driving force and this must involve us, in turn, in discussing the role of political parties in local government.

Notes

1. Although reporting in 1969 the Wheatley Commission made use of a survey of Scottish councillors carried out in 1965.
2. Eversley (1973, p.205) argues that their social origins amongst the petty bourgeoisie are likely to have given them 'a distinctly right wing bias'.
3. Other than those Midland City natives still working there.
4. In 1972 for example social workers demonstrated against Hackney Council over the dismissal of a head of a social work team who had tried to involve clients in the work of the social services department (*Guardian,* 10 February 1972).
5. Cheshire's Chief Executive 'dates his own commitment to the programme (of committee reorganisation) which the council pursued from the meal he shared with the Conservative Whip at a Conference in Harrogate in October 1965' (Lee *et al.,* 1974, p.85).
6. Thus the members and officers of the old Holborn Council regularly met for drinks at the Holborn Golf Circle after meetings (Wistrich, 1972, pp.7-9). Herbert Morrison's political puritanism led him to ban any such fraternisation at the LCC lest it impede the proper conduct of business (Donoughue and Jones, 1973, pp.196-7).
7. Chairmen may of course sometimes collude in such an arrangement.
8. Modified from Friend and Jessop (1969, pp.48-54).

3 PARTY POLITICS

The existence of organised political groups on local councils is no recent phenomenom. It is clear that in the major towns, at least, of the Victorian era, political conflict between various parties, groups and factions was a recurrent event. Indeed Bulpitt suggests that one of the reasons why Parliament was so unwilling to grant many real powers to the reformed municipalities in 1835 was the fear that party considerations were likely to dominate the new corporations (Bulpitt, 1967, p.5). This fear was certainly borne out in Leeds, and in Exeter, for example. Leeds was a battleground for party politics right from the time of the 1835 Act, with vigorous contests between party caucuses for control not merely of the council but of the Poor Law Guardians, of Commissioners elected under local parliamentary Acts, and of various parochial offices, taking place throughout the 1830s and 1840s (Fraser, 1973). In Exeter 'the city council was firmly divided on political lines from the outset and was controlled by the Conservatives for sixty-four years out of seventy-seven between 1837 and 1914' (Newton, 1968, p.302). Other major towns were also the scene of organised political conflict during the first half of the nineteenth century. In Oldham in the three decades up to 1842 a militant working class Radicalism gained control of the local police and of the poor law system and operated them in the interests of local workers (Foster, 1974, pp.56-64). In 1849 the Chartists achieved a narrow but temporary majority amongst the elected councillors (though not among the aldermen) in Sheffield (Hampton, 1970, p.44; Sheffield Trades and Labour Council, 1967, p.5).

The main political issues which found expression in organised conflict in Victorian cities were three in number: education and its relationship to religion; levels of municipal spending; and drink, together of course with the inevitable clashes of personality and factional loyalties. The issue of education expressed itself particularly over the question of the provision and finance of denominational schools and led to contests between Liberal Non-Conformists and Anglican Conservatives for control of the School Boards. When the latter were abolished and education was transferred to the local councils under the 1902 Education Act, the politico-religious enthusiasms were transferred to the councils as well. The debates about municipal spending were essentially between the 'improvers' and the 'economisers'. This distinction between those who wished to finance new facilities and those who wished to retrench did not always fall into identical party alignments. Thus the Conservatives were 'economisers' in Manchester but 'improvers' in Liverpool (Bulpitt, 1967, p.6). Indeed the 'improving' proclivities of Liverpool Conservatives eventually led them to endorse municipal provision of tramways, electricity and even a zoo in the early years of the twentieth century (Petrie, 1972, p.16). In Leicester the fight over spending was fought out, not between the main parties, but within the ranks of the Radical Liberals (Briggs, 1968, p.373). The issue of drink tended to divide local politicians along similar lines to those of religion, with liberal Non-Conformity rallying to oppose the licensed victuallers in the name of teetotalism as they did in Middlesborough at the end of the nineteenth century (ibid., p.259).

Despite the liveliness of many of these local conflicts it was not until the last decades of the nineteenth century that there emerged anything resembling a coherent urban political programme attached to a permanent political organisation. The foundation of the Birmingham Liberal Association in 1865 and its adherence to a programme of municipal reform laid the foundation for Joseph Chamberlain's successful capture of the City Council and the School Board in 1873 (Herrick, 1945; McGill, 1962). Chamberlain's combination of a positive radical policy and a permanent political organisation, the 'caucus', was a new departure. 'Both were wildly controversial. . .City government was never quite the same again' (Briggs, 1968, p.193). The emergence of municipal Socialist ideas in the 1890s in the Labour movement gave added impetus to the growth of a programmatic urban politics.

The heightening of party political activity in urban areas towards the close of the century had its counterpart in the new county authorities first elected in 1889. Party contests occurred in the elections for some fifteen counties, Kesteven, Derbyshire, Warwickshire, Oxfordshire, Hampshire, Devon, Cornwall, Holland, West Riding, Cumberland, Cheshire, Wiltshire, Northamptonshire, Lincolnshire and Durham, plus the new London County Council (Dunrabin, 1965, pp.361-2; Drummond, 1962). Only in London however did party politics persist on any large scale at the subsequent county elections.

At the end of the Victorian era, a basic question in local politics was how far success would attend the attempts by Radicals and the fledgling labour movement to introduce programmatic politics. Thus in Wolverhampton during the years 1898-1902, the initiative in forcing electoral contests came from these quarters in an attempt to oppose the traditional personality-based alliance of Conservatives and Liberals by

means of candidates committed to specific policies of local social reform
(Jones, 1969, p.38).

For the newly formed Labour organisations, such as the Independent
Labour Party and the Social Democratic Federation, local politics
provided a good opportunity for gaining practical experience of
government at a time when national political power seemed a long way
away. Moreover the collective nature of council and committee decision
making ensured that even small Socialist minorities were guaranteed a
voice in the proceedings once elected. The new Labour groups on the
town councils pressed for provision of workers' housing, for better
sanitation, for public baths, for better wages and conditions for the
council's work-force and for the provision of work for the
unemployed. They were primed with advice and information from the
Fabian Society on topics such as housing, education, public health and
the like (Pelling, 1965, pp.157-8).

Although the local government franchise remained still weighted
against the working class, between 1888 and 1894 the creation of new
county councils and urban district councils and the abolition of the
cumulative property vote in elections for the Poor Law Guardians
increased the opportunity to elect working-class candidates. Local
branches of the ILP and the SDF, together with *ad hoc* associations of
Labour supporters and trades councils, contested local elections with
increasing success. Labour gained brief control of West Ham in 1898,
and won Woolwich in 1903. By 1913 Labour candidates were able to
secure net gains of some 200 seats at that year's elections for borough,
district and parish councils and for the Poor Law Guardians (Cole, 1948,
pp.445-6). At the next local elections, after the war, in 1919, the total
net gains by Labour in the provincial and London metropolitan boroughs
alone soared to 938 seats: control was secured of twelve metropolitan
boroughs, the county councils of Durham, Glamorgan and
Monmouthshire, and the city council of Bradford. From that point
onward Labour's place in local government was secure, despite inevitable
ups and downs. By 1939 there were Labour majorities on the LCC, as
well as the three counties won in 1919, on eighteen of the seventy-nine
county boroughs and on seventeen of the twenty-nine metropolitan
boroughs (ibid., pp.447-50 and 458). The anti-Socialist reaction took
varied forms, with candidates emerging under a variety of labels to
contest Labour's incursion into local politics, some standing simply as
Conservatives or Liberals, others representing anti-Socialist caucuses of
differing title and longevity.

The local elections of 1945 saw a repetition of Labour's post-war

successes of 1919 with gains in the provincial and metropolitan boroughs
reaching 1,600 seats (ibid., p.458). Both the Liberal and the Conservative
parties had now recognised the need for a well-organised fight under
their true party colours in the local elections especially in the urban
areas. The consequent decline in successful non-party candidates was
marked. In the various local government elections in the counties and
the urban areas in the ensuing years the Independent[1] candidates suffered
almost continual heavy losses. In England and Wales between 1947 and
1952 an unbroken run of annual net losses totalled some 1,500 seats, and
in the following decade annual net losses totalled over 400 seats to be
offset against the modest gains of 32, 25 and 4 seats in 1955, 1959 and
1960 (Conservative Central Office, Local Government Department:
Local Government Election Results). The net result of these
developments was that by the time the Maud Committee came to
investigate the extent of party involvement in local government they
found that it had penetrated to all but the most rural areas. Less than a
quarter of the rural districts and only a third of the counties operated
on a party basis, compared with more than three quarters of the various
urban authorities. (CMLG, 1967, vol.1, pp.108-9). The new authorities
set up following reorganisation seem likely to be the scene of further
party politicisation of local government. In the England and Welsh
counties the share of Independent seats after the 1973 elections fell
from 40 per cent to 14.3 per cent, with only Cornwall and the Isle of
Wight having an Independent majority amongst the new English
counties. In the non-metropolitan districts of England, Independents
secured only 30 per cent of the seats. In the metropolitan district
elections they could manage on each occasion fewer than 40 seats out
of 2,500 (Municipal Journal, 20 April 1973; 18 May, 1973; 15 June 1973;
9 May 1975). In the elections to the new Scottish authorities the parties
also made advances against the Independents (*Municipal Year Book 1975*,
pp.1324-5 and 1386). This pattern seems likely to continue. Not only
does it represent the result of Labour reaching out from its urban
strongholds into rural hinterlands, after reorganisation, it is also the
outcome of an explicit Conservative policy of encouraging former
Independents of Conservative leaning to stand under the party label or
else face an official Conservative opponent (Allen and Dawson interviews).

The operation of party politics within local government is not of
course something unique to Britain. Robson (1972, pp.83-4) has
observed that it is found in major cities all over the world. In the USA,
in Sweden, in the Netherlands, and in West Germany parties are active
in local government, indeed in Swedish local government 'politics are

all pervasive. . .the non-political member being almost unknown'
(CMLG, 1967, vol.4, p.44). However 'party politics extend to lower
levels of decision-taking in local authorities in England and Wales'
than they do in some other countries and local parties are often
'permanently embattled' in a way that is rare elsewhere (CMLG, 1967,
vol.1, p.106).

Notwithstanding its very long historical pedigree the presence of
party politics in local government is something which arouses misgivings,
even downright hostility, in some quarters. This has perhaps been
especially the case in the years since the First World War whereafter the
gradual extension of the local government franchise to all adults was
followed by the introduction into local politics of mass parties
organised both for electoral and council combat in a manner far different
from the local cliques and factions of Victorian Liberalism and
Conservatism. Briggs points out that democratic urban politics – the
politics of mass opinion and of political organisation – presented a
threat to an earlier deferential politics, to the personal influence of the
local industrialists, the landowners, the squires and the county families.
In rural areas moreover, there was often a long-sustained distrust of the
type of politics and policies emanating from the cities. In the shires the
mass politics and the radical programmes of the Manchester-based
Anti-Corn Law League in the 1840s, or of the Birmingham-based land
campaign of Chamberlain and Collings in the 1880s, appeared to
country society as a threat to the way of life of the landed interests
(Briggs, 1968, pp.65 and 120-1).

Thus hostility to the gradual spread of local party politics from its
Victorian urban strongholds across the nation at large may be seen as
representing not merely a distaste for a particular organisational form
of local politics but also a trepidation as to the content, style and aims
of that form of politics. A similar unease found expression in Germany
where traditional nineteenth-century liberals opposed the growth of a
style of politics in which newly enfranchised groups 'engaged in vigorous
electoral agitation and. . .tried to convert allegiance to a national party
platform into support for local office' (Sheehan, 1971, p.129).
Comparing London, Paris and New York at the end of the last century,
Yearley notes a similar unhappiness on the part of the traditional
'respectable elements' by whom 'the introduction of immigrants,
ignorant or propertyless masses, even workingmen, as the case may have
been, into the inner sanctum of decision, was firmly resisted' (Yearley,
1973, p.57). It is thus arguable that opposition to local party politics
was not simply a rational critique of an operational practice but also

represented a reaction to the loss of power and influence which it might impose on those who had traditionally wielded both, a loss which might be followed by policies and practices inimical to the interests of the 'respectable elements'.

Nevertheless, whatever the motives and interests behind the hostility to local party politics, it remains true that its critics do proffer specific complaints as to just how it fails to meet the needs of local government, and these complaints merit some recognition.

The criticisms generally fall into four types. There is the complaint that channelling candidacies through party organisations leaves the choice in the hands of a few active members, discourages the right sort of people from putting their names forward, and encourages the selection of candidates solely on the basis of their record of party loyalty and service. On the council itself, it is claimed, the existence of party groups stifles free discussion and renders council debates meaningless since all decisions are effectively taken at private group meetings. In terms of policy making the argument is made that doctrinaire party policies are liable to be adopted regardless of individual local circumstances and flying in the face of technical advice from officers. Finally it is alleged that parties promote conflict within the local community and that this is harmful and unnecessary (CMLG, 1967, vol.1, pp.109-10; Grant, 1973, pp.247-9).

This last point is of course crucial and yet imponderable in the sense that ultimately its acceptance or otherwise depends on whether or not one believes in the existence locally of a community characterised by little or no conflict between its component groups. It is of course possible for there to exist small communities based on such a narrow range of social groups that internal conflict is rare: mining villages might present such a close, face-to-face community. However, at the scale of the present local authority, there are bound to be differing social groups living within the same political boundary. The issue then becomes whether the relations between these groups will be marked by consensus or by conflict and whether, if there is conflict, it can be adequately accommodated in a party political format. In practice many of those who abhor the notion of a community characterised by conflict are prepared to concede, at least in the abstract, the reality of conflict at national level in terms of classes or of both sides of industry, and to accept the relevance of party to this national clash of interest. Of course to admit the possibility of such an abstract national clash being reproduced in local reality is to admit that the opposing side is present in flesh and blood, nursing their grievances — real or imaginary —

somewhere nearby, on the other side of town. To those who do well out of the established order, who would like to believe that that order is equally acceptable to others, it may seem inconceivable, or if conceivable, best forgotten, that those who do less well out of it, and are sometimes aware of the fact, are living on the new council estate or in the back street terraces. In this situation the belief in local consensus and in the undesirability of local party politics becomes a shield against unpalatable interpretations of the local social order. The relationship between the ideal of local community consensus and wider social conflict is aptly summed up by Rose (1974b, p.16):

> In England, every individual can identify with two very different groups: the local community in which he lives, and the social class in which his occupation places him. In so far as community identification is more important than nationwide class considerations, one would expect national party labels to have little meaning in local politics. . .This is not the case in Britain.

However, even if one accepts that broadly class-based parties have some relevance to local as well as to national situations because of the ever-present nature of social conflicts, there still remains to be dealt with the criticisms of parties in terms of their impact on candidate selection, on council discussion and debate, and on policy making. Before such criticisms can be dealt with it is clearly essential to examine the way in which parties in fact operate in relation to local government, since a judgement must ultimately be based on an assessment of the actual performance of the local parties.

The Local Parties

In both the major political parties the key unit of local organisation is the parliamentary constituency and below that the local authority ward. Traditionally the winning of seats in Parliament has been the primary objective — at least in the eyes of party headquarters — and thus the constituency rather than the local authority has been the primary point of political reference. A slight move away from this position may now be indicated by the decision of the Labour Party at its 1974 Annual Conference to establish District Labour Parties, aligned with the new local authorities, as well as Constituency Parties, each built up from ward branches within their various boundaries.[2] This represents a more permanent structure for local Labour politics than the ad hoc joint committees which used to operate where local authority boundaries

cut across those of constituencies. In the Conservative Party local
government remains as before the special concern of local government
advisory committees established within the constituency Conservative
Associations.

Individual membership of local Party branches varies, with the
Conservatives averaging about 2,700 members a constituency and Labour
between 500 and 600 (Rose, 1974b, p.157). Active involvement in local
party politics is clearly a minority interest, since by no means all those
who subscribe to a local Party will attend its meetings or be otherwise
actively involved. A survey of one constituency Labour party with just
over 800 members revealed that less than 100 of these were 'activists'
in the sense of regularly attending meetings or taking part in
electioneering (Forester, 1973). Such activists are self-selected by their
own enthusiasms and inclination, and have been seen by some as having
been attracted into politics by zealotry for a particular political doctrine
(cf. McKitterick, 1960). However, this seems on closer examination to
be true of only a vocal minority, with the majority of activists having
views akin to the moderate conventional wisdom of the day rather than
to some ideological extremism (Stack, 1970; Rose, 1962; Rose, 1974b,
ch.VIII). The argument about the activist as ideological militant has
tended to obscure other motivations for political action. The notion that
party workers see themselves solely as links in some national ideological
crusade or as agents of some national election campaign overlooks other
reasons for involvement. In Manchester Bochel found that activists cited
personal and social factors — friendship, helping people, serving the
community or the country — rather than the chance to work for a
cause as the rewards which sustained their activism. Initial motivations
for taking up party work had been a mixture of the political and the
non-political: ideology, personal experiences, influences of friends and
of family (Bochel, cited in Rose, 1974b, p.214). The influence of prior
family involvement as a factor in political activity has been noticed in
Barking and in Glasgow (Rees and Smith, 1964, p.69; Budge *et al.*,
1972, p.32). A survey in four county boroughs in Merseyside found that
officers of ward branches in both the Labour and Conservative parties
saw the branch's main roles as being attending to local needs, and
expressed themselves as having almost as much personal concern over
local as over national issues (Parkinson, 1971). In some cases indeed local
party branches may be almost non-political in their preoccupations,
concerned with questions of procedure and organisation, membership,
finance and social events rather than with major issues of policy (Blondel,
1958; Donnison and Plowman, 1954; Batley, 1972). Birch's observations

on local parties may be still as good a summary of reality as they were when he first made them (Birch, 1959, p.44):

> (They) are self-perpetuating and self-contained, busy with their own affairs, not greatly troubled from day to day by party leaders, party bureaucracy, or even by party policy. . .It would be unwise to be dogmatic about what their business is: sometimes it is local government, sometimes social life, sometimes personal rivalries and ambitions, often a mixture of all three.

It is from these sources, or through these channels, that there emerge the party candidates who contest the local government elections. Both the major parties lay down procedures which should be adopted in selecting local candidates. In the case of the Conservatives individual ward committees may recommend a candidate for their ward to the Executive Council of the Constituency Association: once the Executive Council has approved him he or she may be presented for adoption at a general meeting of ward branch members (Conservative Party, 1971a). In the Labour Party a panel of potential candidates is compiled by the Executive Committee and endorsed by the General Management Committee of the Constituency Party, (or District, County or Regional Party where these are not identical with the parliamentary constituency) from nominations made by ward branches, and other affiliated bodies such as trades union branches and the Women's and Young Socialist groups. Ward branches are then able to select a candidate from the approved panel at a meeting attended by branch members plus representatives of the Executive Committee (Labour Party, 1975).

The rather different procedures outlined above suggest that it is possible for there to be a greater degree of central control over ward selections in the Labour Party than in the Conservative Party. By interviewing — if it so chooses — all would-be nominees, by selective endorsement on to the approved panel, by careful timetabling of the selection meetings in the various wards, and by virtue of having representatives at the selection meetings, the Executive Committee might hope to influence which candidates fought which ward. In practice, the supply of would-be candidates is not generous enough to permit such a degree of picking and choosing and the Executive Committee operates as a formal clearing-house rather than as a master strategist. The extent of central influence on selection is of less consequence than the rather different requirements which the two parties make of would-be candidates.

The Labour Party, being in some ways more single-minded in its devotion to politics than the Conservatives, looks essentially for political experience in its candidates, which means in practice experience within the party, the unions and the co-operative movement. Thus evidence from Manchester, from Wolverhampton, from Camden and from Barking shows that in selecting their potential councillors Labour branch members are likely to prefer those who have held party or union office, done political chores, and sat on the innumerable committees that proliferate throughout the Labour movement (and are perhaps a preparation for the almost as innumerable committees of local government) (Bochel, 1966; Jones, 1969, p.98; Wistrich, 1972, pp.75-6; Rees and Smith, 1964, p.37). Conservatives, however, cast their net wider than their active membership in seeking candidates, drawing in those of sympathetic persuasion who have made themselves known in the social or charitable life of the community. The official injunction that 'many excellent candidates can be found in the various organisations which are carrying on voluntary work in the district' (Conservative Party, 1971, p.4) sums up this approach.

The differing routes to selection within the two parties have certain consequences. One is that the Labour councillor sees a close link between his work for the party and his tenure of a seat on the council. The party has, as it were, groomed him, selected him, financed his campaign, and made it all possible. 'For the Labour Councillor party was essential, beneficial, and loomed large in his life, but for many Conservatives party was a harmful intrusion, one factor in his life among many and not of crucial importance.' (Jones, 1969, p.100.) For the Labour councillor his party has been a source of advancement and of political purpose, for the Conservative councillor, it may have been merely a source of well-earned recognition of a personal worth already established in a non-partisan context. The initially greater identification of Labour councillors with their party should not lead us to suppose however that their Conservative counterparts do not become involved in their own party. Wistrich observes that in Camden the Conservative councillors acquired party office after they joined the council (Wistrich, 1972, pp.75-6). It may thus be the case that the public careers of Labour and Conservative local politicians are differentiated by the manner in which they develop their activities; with Labour politicians initially working within the party, then on the council, and finally, like most senior councillors, acquiring links with voluntary organisations, whilst Conservatives, having started in the voluntary organisations, go on into council work and then into party activity.

Apart from the differing salience of party to councillors there are other consequences of selection by party. Given the small number of activists in any one ward branch it is always possible that the selection process is in effect undertaken by a self-appointed clique. This can be particularly unfortunate in the case of local authorities with only one effective party, since the infusion of new blood and new ideas on to the council then becomes the sole responsibility of that party and its activists. Thus in the old metropolitan borough of Islington, the ruling local Labour Party with its overwhelming majority on the council, was dominated by a small number of local families who fended off outsiders and operated the party and the Group as an almost private fief producing in the end an ageing, introverted and unimaginative council (Butterworth, 1966). Fortunately the new Labour Party Rules go some way to prevent this type of closed selection by involving the Constituency (or District, etc.) Executive Committee in selections where the ward cannot meet an agreed quorum of members. In any event, selection by clique is not purely a party phenomenom. Any private gathering of half a dozen citizens may decide to nominate their own candidate for any one of a dozen reasons, worthy or unworthy, and then go on to cloak him in the respectability of a non-party label.

It is, of course, possible that in selecting a council candidate local party members may be looking for inappropriate qualities. There are few occasions when rank and file activists can exercise any real degree of political power. Resolutions to Annual Conference may be amended or composited out of all recognition and subsequently defeated or, if carried, ignored, whilst choosing a parliamentary candidate is a rare experience in a safe seat and a rather pointless exercise in a hopeless seat. But local elections are fairly frequent and offer prospects of pockets of success even in constituencies which are in total unwinnable. Thus in choosing his candidates for the council the party worker may air all manner of social, political and personal prejudices which find little outlet at other times. The same is true however of those who choose non-party candidates since they are presumably prone to most of the human frailities which impinge on us when selecting our fellows for preferment. In one respect, though, the party workers may be prone to use a particular set of criteria not employed in non-party circles, namely the nominees' views on national political issues. However, it is not self-evidently true that a candidate's position in, for example, general Left-Right terms, is wholly irrelevant to any future decisions he may have to make on for example, secondary education, or housing policy, or levels of expenditure.

The complaint is sometimes made that party selection impedes recruitment of some would-be candidates who find party membership unacceptable. The Social Survey for the Maud Committee however found that only 1 per cent of electors gave this as the main reason why they did not stand for election (CMLG, 1967, vol.3, table 207). It may of course be the case that this 1 per cent includes a high proportion of people of 'the right calibre'. Even so, the evidence of Clements and, of Harrison and Norton, suggests that they are not so much deterred by the need to become party members, which as we have seen need entail no more than a formal allegiance on the Conservative side, as by the fact of having to engage in the hurly-burly of democratic elections plus the prospects of periodic bouts of frustration on the opposition benches (Clements, 1969; CMLG, 1967, vol.5, pp.50-1). Conversely the ability of party organisations to plan and finance a campaign has probably enabled many individuals to stand for the council who would otherwise have lacked the resources to do so: it is certainly the case that the proportion of contested seats, and thus the number of potential councillors, is higher in local authorities organised along party lines than in those where independents dominate (CMLG, 1967, vol.5, p.48). Given the fact that recruitment of council candidates has been a general problem in local politics (CMLG, loc. cit.), it is hard to disagree with the conclusion reached in respect of Glossop by Birch who concluded 'that the membership of the Council is maintained not by the enthusiasm or ambitions of the potential candidates, but by the perserverance of party leaders in seeking candidates' (Birch, 1959, p.123; see also Rees and Smith, 1964, p.76 for similar conclusions in respect of Barking).

Once elected to the council the party's candidates become members of the party Group on the council. At this point there arises the issue of the relationship between the Group and the wider local party in the community. In the case of the Conservative Party, there is little emphasis on formal ties between party and Group. Policy making is the perogative of the Group in the final analysis, although it may be discussed in the Constituency Association's Local Government Advisory Committee if there is one. This Advisory Committee can include Group representatives if the Association wishes but its composition is a matter for the Association to decide. Essentially, these advisory committees are mainly concerned with exchanging information, helping to find and brief candidates, and publicising local Conservative policy, rather than with policy formulation. Constituency Association officers rarely have the right to attend Group meetings, although there is now a growing tendency for constituency agents to act as secretaries of Conservative groups. In essence the Conservative Group can be as autonomous as it wishes since there are no rules limiting its autonomy, nor any procedures laid down whereby those who wished to challenge that autonomy could do so — other than by selecting more pliable candidates at the next elections (Conservative Party, 1971, ch.3; Allen and Dawson Interviews).

The situation inside the Labour Party is much more highly formalised, at least on paper. Nationally the relationship between party members and their elected legislators had been defined in the party's constitution of 1918, albeit in such a way as to leave scope for varying interpretation. No such definition framed the relationship between councillors and their local parties. A series of disputes as to the proper relationship occured during the 1920s. They culminated in a severe crisis in relations between the Liverpool City Council Labour Group and the Liverpool Trades Council and Labour Party which claimed the right to regulate Group business and to discipline Group members. The fact that the Leader of the Group, W.A. Robinson, was a member of the party's National Executive Committee enabled him to raise the matter at this level, with the consequence that a sub-committee was appointed to draft model Standing Orders defining the proper relations of party and Group (Labour Party NEC Minutes, vols. 54, 55, 56, 1930). A significant feature of these Standing Orders was that they restricted the role of non-councillor party representatives at Labour Group meetings to a purely consultative, non-voting one. At the 1930 Party Conference when the Orders were presented for adoption they came under fire from those who thought they allowed the councillors too much leeway. The delegate from Bootle, himself a councillor, commended the practice of his own Trades Council and Labour Party which met monthly 'to discuss the Council agenda and to instruct the members of the local Council as to what they should do', and regretted that the new proposals did not give 'sufficient control of local Labour Groups' to the local party. His complaint was echoed by the delegate from Chorley: '. . .there was not a single thing in the Standing Orders that gave a party control over its Councillors after they were elected'. The Conference however sided with the view of Herbert Morrison that, 'they could not possibly run Local Government on the basis of Councils being marionettes whose actions ought to be decided in detail from outside' (Labour Party Conference Report, 1930, pp.163-5).

The 1930 Memorandum and Standing Orders, amended in 1939, together with the new Party rules adopted in 1974 regulates relations

along the following lines. It is the function of the appropriate local
section of the party (i.e. the Constituency, District, County or Regional
Labour Party) to determine the policy put forward at local elections in
consultation with the Labour Group. The Group determine their policy
and action on the Council within the general lines of the election policy:
the Group also has the duty of deciding on matters not covered by
election policy. For purposes of liaison the party is allowed to send
non-voting representatives to Group meetings, and the Group in turn
should nominate one of its number to report back to the local party.
Thus the relationship is spelt out in some detail. Interestingly enough it
is a relationship which potentially gives the party more control over its
local than over its national politicians at election times. Whereas local
election policymaking is simply the function of the local party, at
national level the election manifesto is prepared by a joint meeting of
the National Executive Committee and the Parliamentary Committee of
the Parliamentary Labour Party and even then they are only committed
to choosing from those policies which secured a two-thirds majority at
the annual Conference. Despite the important role thus given to the
party in local election policy making its members are explicitly warned
that 'attempts to control local administration from outside and to
undermine the public responsibilities of councillors, have proved
disastrous' and that 'under no circumstances must there be any
attempt to *instruct* councillors as to how they should act at group and
council meetings' (Labour Party, n.d., p.2, and 1975, pp.11-12). The
inherent clash between these sentiments and a rigid interpretation of
local party rights has on occasion provided the source of conflict
between party and Group in various local authorities.

Whatever the formal links between local party and council Group in
either the Labour or the Conservative Party, on any given issue of local
importance there are a variety of ways in which the attitudes of the two
sections may relate to one another. It is possible for party and Group to
be at one with one another over an issue, or for them to be at
loggerheads, or for a minority of the Group to appeal to the party over
the heads of the majority of the Group.

The likelihood of party and Group being in agreement, generally or on
specific issues, is of course much enhanced when councillors are also
active members and officeholders in their party. This may be achieved
either by councillors continuing in office or in activism after election to
the local authority or by their taking up party activities subsequent to
their election. Various studies have found a tendency for this
overlapping of councillorship and activism to be a major feature of local

politics especially on the Labour side (Jones, 1969, p.173; Rees &
Smith, 1964, p.57; Baxter, 1972, pp.103-6; Heclo, 1969, p.196;
Butterworth, 1966, p.28; Rose, 1974b, p.173). This may of course lead
to internal party harmony but it can have deleterious side effects. In
Liverpool for nearly two decades after 1945, the Labour Group and the
Labour Party in the city were effectively run by fewer than a dozen
people few of whom had any great interest in local government policy
questions (Baxter, loc. cit.). Where there is effectively a one-party
council the party itself may be the only significant power base from
which effective opposition can arise, albeit internal opposition.
Overlapping in this situation can thus serve to stifle all effective
criticism, as occurred in Islington until massive electoral defeat in 1968
produced the enforced retirement of long entrenched councillors from
both Group and party, to be followed by a youthful insurgency of new
blood (Harrington, 1971).

Where there is a dispute between the local party and all or part of
the Group much clearly depends on the importance of the issue and on
the party within which the conflict occurs. The presumption of
complete Group autonomy on the Conservative side allows them the
last word subject to the perils of seeking readoption at the next
election. On the Labour side it does seem possible in practice for
Groups to withstand almost any amount of pressure if they are so
minded. Thus in Birmingham the Labour Group resisted pressure from
the Borough Labour Party to adopt a policy of comprehensive
education until it became official government policy with the publication
of Mr Crosland's circular in 1965 (Isaac-Henry, 1972, p.32). In Newham
and in Islington both Labour Groups voted in favour of implementing
the 1972 Housing Finance Act despite decisions by local Constituency
Parties that implementation should be resisted. In any event on most
issues it is likely that councillors and party activists will have broadly
similar views: in Camden Wistrich found that the main impact of the
party on Labour councillors was to sustain and reinforce their views
rather than to change them, occasionally nudging them and prodding
them to move faster but enabling the Group to insist on keeping policy
determination 'firmly in its own hands' (Wistrich, 1972, pp.89-90).

To talk of the local party and the council Group as though they
were separate entities may tend to obscure the possibility that both
might be merely manifestations of some tightly-knit local political
organisation akin to the ill-famed machine of American city politics.
Certainly there have been occasions when local political power tended
to coalesce into a small number of hands which controlled both party

and Group. The years when Herbert Morrison ran both the London
Labour Party and the London County Council Labour Group is a case
in point. Yet the evidence here is clearly that such a concentration of
power was not used for venal purposes, and that moreover Morrison
himself combined a puritan political morality with a refusal to accept
that Groups should take detailed instructions from any outsiders
(Donoughue and Jones, 1973, pp.76-7). Under his leadership there was
no question of local politicians being mere errand-boys for outside
interests. Mention has already been made of the tight control exercised
in Liverpool over the Labour Group and the Party (officially the Trades
Council and Labour Party) by a small group of individuals, centred
around John Braddock in the years after 1945. However, the main
consequences of this was largely to channel patronage (e.g. Group
offices and committee chairmanships) into favoured quarters rather
than to permit any depradations upon the public purse or any political
policy extravagances. Indeed the basic characteristic of the Braddock
years was a lack of interest in policy innovation[3] and a concern for
old-fashioned status and prestige (Baxter, 1972). Similarly, in West
Ham, in London, the majority Labour Group, led by Sam Boyce for
three decades from the mid-1930s, largely avoided political principles
as a topic of debate and concentrated on enjoying patronage, power
and prestige. Such a preoccupation with the perquisites of office may
seem both reprehensible and ludicrous to confident critics of established
social position. Yet it may be the case that local politics has provided
the only avenue to a recognition and public status otherwise denied by
society to many manual workers. In a status-conscious society it is
hardly surprising that once attained, it should be clung to for dear life.
It is hard to see in this sort of political formation the characteristics of
the machine outlined by Ostrogorski:

> . . .an aggregation of individuals stretching out hierarchically from
> top to bottom, bound to one another by personal devotion, but
> mercenary, and bent solely on satisfying their appetites by exploiting
> the resources of a political party. (Ostrogorski, 1964, vol.II, p.183).

This description comes nearer to fitting the activities of T. Dan Smith
and his accomplices but their organisation seems to have been not so
much vertical, holding in thrall a town from top to bottom, but
horizontal, depending on judiciously acquired contacts over a variety
of authorities. As yet there is no hard evidence that they were able to
control party offices and council candidacies in true machine fashion

although the political folklore of the North-East admits the possibility.

Perhaps the closest approach ever seen in England to a true urban machine and a true city boss was the organisation of Archibald Salvidge of Liverpool during the first quarter of the present century. Basing himself on the Liverpool Working Men's Conservative Association which came to overshadow the more respectable Constitutional Association, Salvidge secured a complete mastery of local politics and established a considerable reputation as an unparalleled political organiser.[4] He went on to become a leading figure in national Conservative politics and probably the only municipal politician to be made a privy councillor without serving at Westminster. Opinions as to his merits vary: one historian describes him as a man of 'outstanding personal integrity. . .influence and sagacity' (Churchill, 1959, p.133), another as a 'repulsive figure' with 'a hectoring, not to say bullying, manner' (Petrie, 1972, p.14). It is unclear how far he was touched by the financial greed of many of his American city boss counterparts. Certainly no formal accusations were ever brought against him, although J.C.C. Davidson, chairman of the Conservative Party organisation in the years 1927-30 claimed that 'he had. . .taken party funds, and when I accused him of this on one occasion he admitted it and broke down. He was really nothing more than a Tammany Boss in Liverpool. . .' (Rhodes James, 1969, p.117.)[5]

However, despite this comparison with such figures as Boss Tweed of New York it is clear that Salvidge and his organisation differed from those American political machines with which they initially invite comparison. In particular, the traditional American boss and his machine based itself on the needs of the immigrant poor. Indeed the boss himself was often of immigrant origin drawing on the ethnic groups of the city for support and opposed by the upper-class respectability of white Anglo-Saxon Protestantism. Salvidge in contrast was a native of Lancashire, and based his organisation on hostility to the Irish Catholic immigrants of Liverpool rather than on succouring them in return for votes. He fused together an alliance of Protestant working men and Conservative business leaders whose disparate elements were held together by what the *Morning Post* described as 'its tough Orange fibre' (Salvidge, 1934, p.206). The ethos of Salvidge's organisation was summed up by the Liberal C.P. Scott in these words 'Liverpool Unionism is a kind of religious faith. It is really an importation from Belfast and rests on hatred of Rome and of the Irish.' (Quoted in Clarke, 1971, p.52.)

Thus the most likely candidate for the role of a city boss in English politics may be seen as a unique phenomenom, resting on an adaptation of Ulster politics to the particular local demands of an urban Conservatism faced with the growth of the Labour movement.

The absence of any other comparable boss or machine in British local politics is probably due to the structure of local government itself. The key function of the American boss and his organisation has been to centralise the 'scattered fragments of power' that has dispersed among the many decentralised institutions of urban government in the United States and to satisfy the material needs of various subgroups which remained unmet through the official channels (Merton, 1957). The more unified nature of British urban government especially in the form of the county boroughs and Scottish counties of cities obviated the need for such a 'shadow' government as the machine could and did provide across the Atlantic. Instead effort could be concentrated on winning control of the local authority through conventional politics. Hence the politicisation of the Irish immigrant took place not through the construction of their own organisations, but through participation in and sometimes (e.g. Liverpool, Islington, Bermondsey at various times between the 1930s and the 1960s) eventual control over the local Labour Party and its traditional operations.

In the absence of any powerful boss figures on the American scale the question of how far councillors are manipulated by political forces outside the council resolves itself into two main questions. One concerns party influence on candidacies, the other party influence on policy. As we have seen, in both the Conservative and Labour parties the selection of council candidates rests with the party members. Given that such people are unlikely, for understandable reasons, to campaign for those whom they dislike or disagree with there is always the possibility that councillors who displease will not be re-adopted. However, the shortage of potential replacements may inhibit the too frequent use of this particular weapon. So, too, may fear of disrupting the social harmony of the small-scale community of activists and local politicians on which ward organisation depends: whereas a sacked MP can be bade good-bye, a sacked councillor, his family and his friends have to be lived with day by day in the locality and in the party. Lack of any practical alternative to the sitting councillor, and fear of disrupted relationships can be powerful inducements to broad-mindedness amongst local activists to whom politics is a practical business and a form of socialising rather than an ideological crusade.

As for control of policy we have seen that whereas there is a presumption of Group autonomy on the Conservative side, in the

Labour Party, if only at election time, the activists are placed in a strong
position, at least on paper. Yet if councillors are at a disadvantage
vis-à-vis council officers, so too are activists *vis-à-vis* councillors who
may claim, correctly, to know more about the practicabilities and
legalities of policy proposals in a local government context than do their
lay comrades. In any case, not only is policy to be made in consultation
with the Labour Group, councillors as individual party members can
and do secure election to the policy making Management Committees.
Thus it would be wrong to see Labour councillors as merely passive
recipients of election policies laid down at meetings beyond their
influence. The notion of the councillors as the mere mouthpiece of the
party activists is as inaccurate as would be the reverse image of the
party activists as the mere electoral machine of the councillors. Both
groups have to live with one another within the framework of their
pretensions to internal party democracy. The conflicts that thereby
may arise from time to time are endemic in any attempt to combine
democratically elected public representatives with democratically run
political parties. If both these latter are thought desirable then the
conflicts are inevitable whether the arena be local or national politics.

Parties on the Council

It is the common practice of Labour, Liberal and Conservative
councillors to organise themselves into party Groups on their local
authorities. The purpose and character of these Groups tends to vary,
not merely as between parties, but from one local authority to another.

On the Conservative side the traditional view of the role of the
Group has been expressed thus:

> The formation of groups which meet regularly to formulate policy,
> discuss tactics and pass information to all members of the group,
> particularly concerning the business of committees of which they are
> non-members is very desirable. This need not interfere in any way
> with the individual opinions of the members who are still entitled
> to freedom of thought and action. If group rules are to be drafted
> let them be of the minimum and regarded as for their own guidance,
> and not be subject to penalties. (Brabin, 1961, p.11.)

In line with this philosophy, Group organisation is the responsibility of
the Conservative councillors themselves and need not follow any
prescribed pattern. Although a brief guide to Group organisation is
made available by Conservative Central Office it is purely advisory and

has no status in the party constitution and indeed merits no mention in the Central Office publication on local government and party organisation (Allen Interview; Conservative Party, 1971a).

The distinction between this position and that of the Labour Party is clearly demonstrated by the existence of Model Standing Orders for Labour Groups and by the observation in the memorandum that accompanies them to the effect that 'essentially the Group must know its own collective mind and work as a Group. . . .Members are expected to abide by Group decisions and not speak or vote in opposition in the Council, unless the Group has decided to leave the matter to a free vote.' (Labour Party, n.d., pp.1 and 2.) The Labour predeliction for this form of organisation derives partly from traditions of solidarity and collective action in the wider Labour movement but also from a conception of the party as the 'battering-ram' of social change having to place all its concerted strength against selected targets in order to effect the innovations it seeks. It is clearly an unnecessary form of organisation for a Conservative Party with the considerable inertia of the status quo on its side. The details of the Standing Orders can be modified at will to suit local requirements subject to approval by the party's National Executive Committee. In practice the operation of Labour Groups varies considerably from authority to authority. Some will adhere closely to the Standing Orders, others will be guided by habit and traditional practice rather than by the written text. Some will operate a tightly whipped system, others will follow Transport House's periodic pleas for avoiding excessive rigidity, others again will rarely take a binding Group decision at all. In general terms however it is probably true that the arrival of Labour on the local government scene, whilst it did not herald the advent of party politics which already existed, did change the style of local politics by introducing the notion of collective party decision making and collective party responsibility along with their accompanying sanctions. Bulpitt suggests in particular that the nature of political conflict on a council may well be a function of how strictly the Labour Group is organised and of how far, in consequence, the other Groups feel obliged to respond in kind. (Bulpitt, 1967, p.120).

Clearly Group organisation and procedures are not ends in themselves. The remarks of Herbert Brabin quoted previously indicate some possible functions which the Groups may perform, namely those of formulating policies, discussing tactics and exchanging information. To these might be added the function of securing the adoption of policies by the council, of co-ordinating individual policies and of scrutinising existing policies and practices. The extent to which individual Groups aspire to, and accomplish, any of these functions will depend on a variety of factors. Thus securing the adoption of desired policies requires an ability to command votes in council and Committee, and hence assumes some degree of discipline within the Group. Formulating policies (as distinct from adopting those proffered by the officers of the local authority) presupposes the opportunity for at least some members of the Group to get away from the day-to-day business of agendas and minutes and to devote time to looking ahead and thinking in longer term perspectives. It may also require access to expert advice over and above that proffered by the officers. The necessary time and advice is not always readily to hand and it is all too easy for Groups to content themselves with a quick run through the next agenda and to avoid the complexities of policy planning. This is particularly true where policy planning involves consideration of documents such as budget proposals, structure plans, or transport policies and programmes. Their sheer bulk and complexity defeats many councillors and even entire Groups, reducing them to uttering vague generalities or riding particular hobby-horses.

A survey of the Majority (Labour) Group on the ILEA from 1970 to 1973 showed that its members rarely discussed future educational policy at Group meetings, which were dominated by questions of current educational practice and procedural matters. Even when policy was discussed nearly one quarter of the discussions revolved around the issue of whether or not the Group should have a policy of its own rather than merely accept the papers supplied by the officers. Attempts to encourage policy planning by setting aside extraordinary Group meetings for this purpose and holding weekend policy conferences failed to attract much more than half the members of the Group (Benn, 1974). In his own study of parties in the North-West, Bulpitt concluded that Labour's attempts to use its Groups as policy making bodies were met by 'few signs to indicate that any such group was particularly successful in its efforts' (Bulpitt, 1967, p.121). The Majority Labour Group in Wolverhampton 'did not initiate or formulate policy. . .it did not look ahead and plan for the future: it was a "hand to mouth" affair living from agenda to agenda' (Jones, 1969, pp.175-6).

Not all groups will operate with quite the same disregard for policy initiatives. In Leeds both the Majority and Minority Groups were each found to have an Advisory Committee which acted as a source of policy ideas (Hill, D.M., in Sharpe, 1967, p.146), whilst Harrison and Norton found that despite an apparently well-merited general scepticism as to the extent to which Groups as a whole could initiate policy, nevertheless in some authorities operating on party lines the party group 'makes a more significant contribution than any single "constitutional" committee towards general policy initiation' (CMLG, 1967, vol.5, pp.105-7 and 193-4). Clearly however the evidence suggests that we cannot automatically assume that all Groups are able or inclined to formulate policies.

Where they do not do so certain consequences may follow, especially where, despite the lack of concern for policy, the majority Group can be tightly organised by appeals to mutual loyalty in a competitive inter-party situation. Under such conditions the Majority Group may become simply a mechanism for securing political approval of the officers' ideas; this is not to say that the officers may not deliberately 'trim' their proposals to suit what they regard as the political predilections of the ruling Group. Alternatively, the Group may become little more than an *ex post facto* guarantor of committee decisions. Thus in Hull committee decisions, often the result of a cross-party vote or an all-party consensus, once reported to the pre-council meeting of the Majority Labour Group, became Group policy unless specifically amended or rejected (Brier, 1970, p.156). In both these situations the majority Group becomes in effect little more than the guarantor of other people's proposals, be it the officers or some bi-partisan committee of the Council.

Where the Groups do attempt to devise policies of their own, certain problems must be overcome. The group itself is likely to be too large, and not able to meet frequently enough, to do the job itself. Thus policy initiation may well fall on the shoulders of an inner caucus of senior members. These may be an informal group of those with the time and inclination to deal in such matters or a special sub-committee of the Group. This produces a situation akin to that of Parliament where the main policy initiatives lie with the Cabinet rather than with the back-benchers, although in the case of the Council Group it is not axiomatic that the policy making caucus will include all the committee chairmen as the Cabinet parallel might suggest.

The making of policy by party Groups does pose a problem also of how far this can be done in the absence of officers' advice, since it has been normal practice for officers not to attend Group meetings. The Bains and Paterson reports however approved the notion of developing mechanisms that would allow party groups to receive official advice. There are of course ways and means to achieve this. Officers can prepare papers for committee chairmen in the knowledge that the contents will be divulged to the ruling Group, or officers can advise a one-party Policy Committee of the Council. Unfortunately, the first method prevents members from cross-questioning the officer, and both methods offer no help to a minority Group. The simplest answer seems to be the practice agreed in Nottinghamshire where officers of the county council may accept or seek invitations to meetings of party Groups but where neither politicians nor officers can compel an officer's attendance. It may still remain a matter for argument as to how far officers can advise the Minority Group outside the formal committee structure without getting dragged into the party battle.

Once one moves away from the matter of Groups as policy makers to that of Groups as scrutineers of current policy and practice, one is in practice talking of Groups as the vetters of committee minutes or reports since it is these which contain the material most readily available for scrutiny. In some cases the party representatives on each committee will hold their own Group meetings prior to the committee meeting to see whether the agenda contains any business meriting a Group decision on the committee. This at least has the merit of reducing the likelihood that when the committee reports to the full council meeting its recommendations will be overturned as unacceptable by the Majority Group on the council — unless there is a conflict between the full Majority Group and its members on a particular committee. Concentrating on the agendas of committees and council meetings rather than on policy initiation certainly enables Group members to acquaint themselves in detail with the on-going work of authority. This forms a major contribution to keeping members informed on the work of all the committees. It also enables individual members to press upon their political colleagues the needs and interests of particular groups in the community affected by individual proposals. Thus in Coventry Friend and Jessop found that the Group was the scene of 'the most persuasive advocacy of the interests of particular sectors of the community — whether school children, old people, ratepayers, tenants of municipal housing, or residents of some particular neighbourhood or street. There was a constant sense of the direct exposure of the elected member to the many conflicting pressures of the electorate.' (Friend and Jessop, 1969, p.58.) Vetting committee reports also provides an opportunity for co-ordinating policies emanating from individual committees, although this presupposes the development by the Group of criteria by which to assess the need for co-ordination and the direction it should take.

It is probably a fair summary to say that as currently constituted, party Groups provide a useful means of exchanging information between members, of pleading cases before a sympathetic audience, and, if effectively organised, of securing the passage through committee and full council of approved recommendations, whatever their source. They also serve to encourage debate and criticism by the mere fact of their organised existence and to ensure, through the existence of Minority Groups, that local government enjoys the equivalent of a Parliamentary Opposition committed:

> ... to state the case against the administration; to say everything which may plausibly be said against every measure, act, or word of every member of the Ministry; in short to constitute a standing censorship of the government, subjecting all its acts and measures to a close and jealous scrutiny. (Alpheus Todd, quoted in Hanham, 1966, p.36.)

They find it more difficult to operate as co-ordinating devices and as policy initiators. To some extent the current development of policy committees reflects an attempt to fill this vacuum where Groups have failed to do so. A key question in the future of local government party politics is whether an effective policy making role for the Groups, and the parties they represent, can be developed.

Thus far we have examined the party Groups largely in terms of their functions within the wider context of the local authority. But something should be said of Groups as political institutions, with their own internal problems of leadership, of conflict and of securing consensus. The internal political structure of a Group will vary according to its size and also, probably, according to whether or not it is in a Majority position on the council. A large Group will be harder to organise, especially on a geographically large authority and this may require for instance assistant whips as well as a chief whip: of course a large Group may also need to accommodate more people eager for Group office than a small Group. Majority Groups have to cope with the problem of relating their own internal political arrangements of office holding with those of the council and its committees. A number of questions are thus posed and they admit of varying answers. Shall the Leader of the Group also be Chairman of the Group or does this give him too much control over Group debate? Shall the Leader hold any committee chairs? If so, shall it be that of any specific committee, such as the central policy committee? Shall the Leader appoint the committee chairmen or should they be elected by Group members?

Shall there be a Group policy committee: if so, whom does it include? Group Officers? Committee Chairmen? Member's of the Council's Policy Committee? Back-bench councillors? How long do the various officers serve?

Little is known of how Groups resolve these questions. There are certain plausible best practices which may be adopted, such as separating the chairmanship and leadership of the Group to prevent the Leader being excessively dominant in debate, or insisting on the major chairmen being on any Group policy committee in order to draw on their knowledge and advice, or making the Leader also chairman of the council's policy committee so that he can effectively lead the council in the direction chosen by the Group. In the last analysis however, the distribution of Group officers and committee chairmanships is not solely a matter of good management but also of good politics and the requirements of good politics depend on political circumstances.

Harrison and Norton concluded that in general party Groups were more likely to throw up 'a group of influential members than a single autocrat' (CMLG, 1967, vol.5, p.112). They also attach some significance to personality as a factor in styles of leadership (ibid., p.111). The notion of Group leadership being in practice a collective rather than an individual function is clearly plausible given the fact that the individual committees give their chairmen a power base of their own with direct access to members and chief officers. As to personality the individual role of Leader can be played as little more than one of spokesman on the floor of the council chamber, or alternatively as a prime mover on major policy issues; these may clearly appeal to different personalities. Given the general difficulty that Groups experience in handling policy formulation, it is not unreasonable to suppose that, personality notwithstanding, many Group Leaders are likely to find themselves primarily occupied as spokesmen, negotiators and reconcilers rather than as policy leaders.

One of the functions of Group leadership must be to maintain the unity of the Group. In some ways of course this will maintain itself without undue effort. A community of values or of social background will sustain the Group at most times. This will probably be reinforced by the mere existence of the opposing Group against whom a united front may be sought. Moreover, many members of the Group will accept the need to 'go along' with their colleagues on a given issue in the expectation that the favour will be reciprocated later on: that, after all, is part of the business of constructing democratic majorities. There will of course be varying individual attitudes within any given

Group. Corina identifies five different types of Group member: the party politician, seeing the Group as a means to achieve his political goals, prepared to take the long view, to compromise, to stick it out; the ideologist, of strong, sometimes rigid conviction, willing to pursue his views to the point of uncompromising opposition; the partyist, with no clear political goals other than total loyalty to the party; the associate who 'keeps his head down' on ideological issues and uses the party for some special interest of his own, such as care of the elderly or child welfare; and the politico-administrator who is likely to be a senior councillor, in good standing with the officers and concerned with expediting the council's business and laying down the law to back-bench members of the Group (Corina, 1974). Such varying attitudes contain within them the seeds of conflict. So too do social, rather than personal characteristics. Groups may contain divisions based on class, on age, on geography, on ideology, on religion. Thus there can be a considerable potential for conflict if a suitable issue arises to provide the occasion if not the cause. It seems likely that this will be specially true of Labour Groups in view of (a) their commitment to discipline which can crystallise conflict as well as resolve it; (b) the availability within the party's constitution of procedures for pursuing internal disputes by appeal upwards through the party organisation; (c) their more ideological style of politics; and (d) the tendency for their membership to be more socially heterogeneous than are Conservative Groups. The lack of any formal mechanisms for discipline or dispute resolution in the Conservative Party as far as councillors are concerned ensures that any disputes which may occur are dealt with by informal pressures and are waged less openly when they occur.

The Impact of Party

Given the fact that parties do operate in local government, and that there is every likelihood of their continuing to do so, it is of some importance to establish the impact which they make on the work of the local authorities. In particular the question arises as to how far the parties justify their local existence by pursuing distinctive policies when in control of a council. This question may be considered in two contexts, how the parties run the council and the policies which the council pursue when under their control.

In terms of council procedure Boaden in his study of county boroughs found that the existence of a Labour majority was associated with speedy transaction of business in short council meetings, with little attempt by the full council to alter committee recommendations, with few items being referred back for further consideration and with few questions put to committee chairmen. In addition there was restricted admission of the public to committee meetings, less ready availability of council documents to the Press, and a low attendance of the public at council meetings. (Boaden, 1971b, pp.112-4.) In addition, a re-analysis of material gathered by Harrison and Norton suggested that Labour councils were much more prone to limit the autonomy of officers and to involve the councillors in questions of detail (Boaden, 1971a, p.422).

Boaden has argued that Labour's swift dispatch of council business reflects a commitment to effective party control 'likely to have been created with policy objectives in mind.' (Boaden, 1969). Regardless of whether policies are initiated by the Group or taken up by the Group from the officers' reports, Labour's belief in a positive role for government encourages Labour Majority Groups to seek speedy implementation of proposals once they have been discussed and accepted in party group meetings. As for attitudes to the respective roles of officers and councillors:

> The typical Conservative approaches his council work with the analogy of private industry in mind: the officers are well paid executives who should be allowed to get on with the job: if they fail then the councillors (board of directors) should hold them to account. . .The typical Labour councillor on the other hand is concerned with the detailed application of policy as well as with the overall success or failure of the enterprise. (Hampton, 1972, p.27.)

This difference of perspective on the importance of detail and on the need to keep the officers on a tight rein, may reflect the fact that by and large the day-to-day impact of local authority services is simply greater on the average Labour voter than on his Conservative counterpart.

Turning to the question of local authority policies, the question arises as to how far these can be said to reflect the differing views of the parties in control. Providing an answer to this question is no easy matter. Different local authorities contain within their boundaries widely varying communities with differing needs and differing resources. The public expenditure needs of an urban industrial authority may be high, those of an established residential suburb comparatively low; some areas of poor housing have low rateable values while others with more substantial properties are blessed with a firmer base for local rating. It could thus be argued that it is socio-economic structure rather

than political attitudes which determine such policies as levels of
expenditure or of the rate levy. Such was the conclusion drawn by
Oliver and Stanyer from a study of county boroughs (Oliver &
Stanyer, 1969). Yet Alt reaches rather different conclusions in a
similar study, showing that Labour control is associated with higher
levels of expenditure on education, housing and local health services
(Alt, 1971). It must not be forgotten that socio-economic structures do
not in themselves generate policies. The generation of policies demands
an ability, or a willingness to recognise needs and to meet them. Thus
Alt observes that whilst needs may well be related to local structural
characteristics, 'it is equally possible that party control can have
independent effects on the perception of needs' (Ibid., p.61). It
certainly appears to be true that party can affect perceptions of needs
and of the proper way to meet them. Thus Jones found that amongst
councillors in Wolverhampton, the Conservatives 'disliked their rates
being used to finance for others services which very often they have
provided for themselves independently', whilst Labour in contrast
'welcomed the redistributive effect of using the rates from the richer
groups to finance services for the poorer' (Jones, 1969, p.321). This
dichotomy of attitudes was confirmed by a former Conservative Leader
on the LCC who saw Conservatives as 'trustees for the contributors of
the money which it is their duty to spend' as distinct from the Labour
inclination towards 'using the rate fund to further the redistribution of
wealth' (Brooke, 1953, p.183). In his study of Conservative councillors
in Kensington and Chelsea Dearlove found them to possess a series of
characteristic views on local government's proper duties: they saw many
local problems as yielding to self-help, they worried over the burden of
rates on the householder, they believed in charging full user costs for
housing and car parking, and they objected to controls (over parking
for example) and to public provision in excess of basic 'housekeeping'
functions such as lighting, sewerage, police, open spaces, pollution
control and public health (Dearlove, 1973, ch.10).

   Traditionally, Labour entered local councils committed to certain
distinctive types of policy. Thus in the early years of Labour
representation in local authorities they were the champions of the
municipal workmen in disputes over wages and conditions of work, as
well as being the advocates of sanitary, housing and welfare developments,
direct works, and municipal trading. Between the wars, Labour
councillors sought the provision of local authority work for the
unemployed. A survey in the 1930s found that Labour control was
associated with more generous public assistance benefits, with more

extensive maternity and child welfare services, and with higher educational expenditure per child (McHenry, 1938, pp.212-4).

Given these party differences as to what local authorities ought properly to do it would be no surprise to discover that the two parties have contrasting perceptions of need and that this contrast will be reflected in the policies favoured by the parties. From his study of county boroughs in England and Wales, Boaden concluded that:

> Councillor disposition measured in party terms was most relevant. . .Labour councils were more active in services with a significant impact on the overall role of government. They were bigger spenders on the bigger services. In addition they were more active where the service appeared to benefit sections of the community supporting them. Even where these two factors were less operative there was a tendency for Labour to favour higher standards in the broadest sense. (Boaden, 1971b, p.112.)

In terms of particular services Boaden found Labour was likely to spend more on education than were other parties whatever the context of need, was more likely to submit plans for secondary school reorganisation along comprehensive lines, and showed a distinct tendency to build more council houses and to pay higher rate subsidies on housing. Similarly, Davies and his colleagues have identified a clear relationship between the extent of Labour representation and certain variables in the levels of welfare provision. Thus in terms of children's services Davies comments on the link between Labour representation and a 'protective' attitude to children in care (Davies, B., 1972, p.110). It seems possible on the available evidence to hazard the general conclusion that at any given level of need party control is the main factor in determining the response to those needs.[6]

The importance of party in determining the range and quality of service does not necessarily extend to all activities of the council. Thus, there seems to be little relationship between party control and for example the readiness to promote private Parliamentary Bills in the areas of public health, planning and environmental control (Scarrow, 1971, pp.13-14). In practice, not every issue that comes before the council will fall neatly along the party divide any more than those which come before Parliament. In some cases the divide will fall within a party Group rather than between Groups. Thus for example, the key battles on the implementation of the 1972 Housing Finance Act were often conducted within Labour Groups rather than between Labour and the

Conservatives. In some cases, the battle over comprehensive education has been fought out within a Majority Group – Labour or Conservative – with the Minority Group hoping for one particular faction to triumph. Nevertheless, despite many issues being tackled on a non-party or cross-party basis, there are some issues which do arouse party passions. In Camden these issues included levels of expenditure, the housing programme, rents, compulsory purchase, direct labour and municipal catering (Wistrich, 1972, p.102). Other issues which from time to time lead to inter party disputes include education, and certain aspects of planning. Over a two-year period from 1973 to 1975, the Essex County Council divided on party lines over such issues as education policy, consumer protection policy, library fines and charges, the alignment of the A12 by-pass, the siting of the Third London Airport, admission of the public to meetings, and the compilation of a register of members' interests. This division reflected partly a division between 'ins' and 'outs' as to the merits of established procedures but also some real divisions as to the proper role of local government, the extent of its responsibilities, and the perception of whose interests within the community stood most in need of defence.

Thus division between the parties, when it does occur, which is not all the time, relates to some fundamental issues which cannot be brushed aside, issues of basic local government policy and also of the defence of the different interests for which the parties stand and by which they are sustained.

Divisions in the Community

The political debate that takes place locally between the parties although it is confined to a small minority of participants, does nevertheless articulate, albeit imperfectly, some of the real divisions of interests and opinion which exist in the local community at large. To those who see their community as being essentially united, and free from the sharp conflicts of national politics, the existence of such divisions is an unpalatable notion.

Nevertheless, the evidence is clear. For one thing the pattern of urban and industrial development together with the policies and preferences of local authorities, building societies, and private house buyers have contributed to a steady geographical segregation of working-class and middle-class groups in the community. The process began during the nineteenth century (Briggs, 1968, p.64) and has continued in the twentieth. The council estate and the private development have become separate worlds, sometimes living in a state

Party Politics   89

of mutual suspicion and antagonism (Collison, 1963). Even in a mixed,
affluent suburb of outer London, Willmot and Young concluded:

> If middle-class people have friends they are usually middle-class too;
> if working-class people have friends they are usually working-class
> too. There were still two Woodfords in 1959 and few meeting-points
> between them. (Willmott and Young, 1960, p.122.)

Given the link between social class and voting habits, the polarised
social geography of class naturally has its political consequences. It
creates safe wards based on large tracts of one class housing and their
residents. In some cases it creates virtually one-party authorities such as
the Labour strongholds of East London and South Wales or the
Conservative seaside towns of southern England. Moreover, geographical
segregation merely compounds and complements segregation at work
and at play. The result is the sort of social and political division
observed by Jones in Wolverhampton:

> . . .the division between Labour and Conservative members (of the
> Council) is not merely a political or even an occupational division,
> but a social one too. . . .each group inhabiting its own world and only
> coming together on the Council (Jones, 1969, p.147.)

Councillors from these two worlds enjoy links with very different local
groups. Conservatives are often involved with religious, charitable and
commercial organisations combining 'good works' and sociability. On
the Labour side, the charitable concept of good works may smack too
much of patronage: here sociability and public service are expressed
through activity within the trades unions, the Labour Club, the WEA,
the Co-operative Education Committee, and the tenants' associations
rather than the Anglican Church, or Rotary or Round Table (Bealey
et al., 1965, pp.362-3; Jones, 1969, pp.134-5; Wistrich, 1972, p.76;
Stacey, 1960, pp.48-51; Stacey *et al.,* 1975, ch.4).

There are of course subdivisions even within these two local worlds.
In some areas of the commuter belt for example the world of middle-
class Conservatism may be split by conflicts between the genteel
paternalism of rural Toryism and the more abrasive managerialism of
the ex-urban commuter. In working class areas particular sub-groups
may dominate local politics, such as the dockers in Bermondsey or the
railwaymen in West Ham. On the Labour side, in particular, there may
be occasional divergences between the perceptions of working-class

activists and those of their middle-class comrades (Hindess, 1971).
Nevertheless, despite such local variations there is much truth in the
notion that locally, as well as nationally, the two major parties
represent distinct sets of supporters living different lives and bringing
different values and experiences to bear on local problems and their
solutions. Moreover, for most of the population, these values and
experiences which they share with their social peers across the country
are more relevant criteria for political judgement than the geographical
accident of residence within the boundaries of a given local authority.
There are indeed social divisions locally, but they are part of a wider
national division. In this sense a major part of local politics is, rightly or
wrongly, a component part of a larger conflict fought out on the
national level; and, as we shall see, this in turn has important
consequences for local electoral behaviour.

In Defence of Parties

The battle of the parties on the local authority is not a mere charade.
Enough has been said to show that their conflict does represent a
genuine disagreement as to what councils should do, how they should
do it, and whose interests and values should be advanced. Moreover,
with formal powers dispersed amongst the various committees and
sometimes delegated to chairmen, and with individual councillors able
to sink their own responsibility in the wider corporate responsibility of
the council as a whole, 'party organisation in council has the great merit
of identifying responsibility for policy and action' (CMLG, 1967, vol.5,
p.398; see also Dunsire, 1956, and Kantor, 1974). Party can thus impart
a sense of direction and purpose to the disparate activities of the various
committees and departments, and can provide the officers with some
form of guidance as to what proposals are likely to meet with
acceptance. In short party provides a common frame of political
reference for the officers, and a common source of information,
inspiration and allegiance for the councillors, thereby unifying an
otherwise fragmented pattern of government.

Outside the council itself parties are also important as a means of
organising local elections and mobilising the vote, and in particular as a
mechanism of recruitment into the ranks of councillors. In the absence
of parties in local elections the consequences may be those experienced
in the United States:

In most situations in which parties have been abolished in municipal
elections, the conservative forces of the community have won most

elections. In the absence of a party based on the lower strata, which could define issues that appealed to their interests and bring them to the polls. . .the voting portion of the electorate in such elections is disproportionately composed of the more privileged. . . . (Lipset, 1964, vol.I, p.lxi; see also Adrian, 1952.)

The role of parties in ensuring the widest use of the electoral process is crucial. At the national level more than half of the seats in Parliament were uncontested prior to the emergence of national parties (Lloyd, 1965). The same problem has already been mentioned in the local context, where the evidence suggests that 'competition for seats is strongest in urban areas and appears to bear a relationship to the presence of party organisations' (CMLG, 1967, vol.5, p.48). With larger authorities and larger electoral areas the importance of party as a means of enabling individuals to wage a local campaign seems likely to increase rather than to decrease. This is particularly true for working-class candidates, for whom parties are in any case the chief avenue of recruitment to the council chamber.

Beyond their periodic function of recruiting candidates and organising election campaigns, parties also serve to some degree to aggregate the various interests within the community. The close links, personal and organisational, between the parties and differing local social and economic groups, enable the parties to receive and absorb the demands of such groups and to carry them into the policy making process. This may help to account for the comparatively modest degree of independent pressure group activity at the local level in Britain compared with the United States.

Political parties then represent genuine divergences of view, they give coherence to the work of local authorities, they function as a means of political recruitment and election organisation, and they represent the demands and interests of differing social groups both organised and unorganised. This much at least may be said in their defence. It still remains to be seen in later chapters how far they are able to function adequately as devices for securing accountability to the voters and as sources of political initiatives.

Notes

1. The figures for Independent candidates here refer to those who stood without any Conservative support in the eyes of Central Office.
2. In addition County and Regional parties were set up to cover the English and

Welsh Counties and the Scottish Regions.
3. Braddock was described by one of his senior officers as 'a pragmatist, with a considerable suspicion of intellectuals and professionals' and thus liable to be hostile to any notions of 'sophisticated planning' (Amos, 1973, p.182).
4. As well as being Conservative Leader on the City Council, he was able to control the selection of parliamentary candidates to the point where most of Liverpool's Conservative MPs were 'genial nonentities who were prepared to knuckle under to Salvidge' (Clarke, 1971, p.233).
5. In fairness, it needs to be said that there was clearly a mutual antipathy between the two men; Salvidge for example describes Davidson as 'fluttering' around Baldwin 'like an admiring hen' (Salvidge, 1934, p.302).
6. As indicated earlier, this in itself does not resolve the question of how far Majority Groups initiate the policies they pursue, as distinct from adopting policies prepared by officers with the party's known attitudes in mind.

4 POLITICS OUTSIDE THE PARTIES

Political parties, especially under a two party system, are essentially broad-based coalitions. As such they may be unable to single out for attention individual issues or interests which may be the active concern of a minority in the community but towards which much of the population is indifferent. Thus those with particular interests to defend, or with specific policies to press on a given issue, are liable to regard the political parties as inadequate vehicles for their purpose. They may also regard 'party' and 'politics' as being in some way irrelevant or even harmful to the cause they wish to plead. Accordingly, they may find it advantageous to create their own vehicle, or organisation, with the aim of either doing themselves what they think should be done or of persuading the appropriate authorities to take the desired action. If they are concerned with persuading authority to act, then clearly they are in the business of attempting to influence the actions of government, even if they do so at one remove by bringing influence to bear on public opinion and on the political parties. Even if they are primarily concerned with taking action themselves they may well seek to influence government in search for example of financial assistance, or of legal enactments encouraging the further development of their activities, or of some modest degree of official recognition for the worth of their work; they may even hope to persuade government to make them redundant by taking on the job itself.

Conventionally organised groups, other than political parties, which seek to influence government decisions are referred to as pressure groups. The literature on pressure groups is at some pains to distinguish between political parties and pressure groups, although the definitions employed may vary somewhat. Thus one definition sees a pressure group as 'any organised group which attempts to influence government decisions without seeking itself to exercise the formal powers of government' (Moodie and Studdert-Kennedy, 1970, p.60): here the crucial characteristic is that a pressure group denies itself any pretensions to a governmental role. Another definition however refers to pressure groups in terms of their not being a political party 'in the sense of being represented. . .in the legislative body' (Castles, 1967, p.1): here the emphasis is not merely on lacking any governmental responsibility, but on lacking any role as a source of elected representatives, whether in government or not.

There are certain problems however about applying these definitions to local politics. For one thing the gulf between the single-minded concern of a pressure group and the manifold wider preoccupations of Government is less at the local level, where many issues — of economic policy, or of foreign affairs — are beyond the scope of local government. A single issue which is one of a multitude at central government level may be one of a few at the local level. Given particular circumstances it may loom sufficiently large to obliterate other issues for a time. When that happens it is a possible tactic for a single-issue pressure group to contemplate contesting local elections and aiming for at least some degree of participation in local government decision making. Thus for example in the late 1960s in Wilmslow, Cheshire, candidates on an 'anti-overspill' ticket fought and won several seats on a programme of opposition to proposals for siting a Manchester overspill estate at Wilmslow (Lee *et al.*, 1974, p.46). In the 1970 GLC elections, 85 candidates from the Homes Before Roads group contested seats in 27 boroughs on a platform of opposition to the GLC's motorway plans, whilst in the London Borough elections of 1974 candidates from the environmentalist Save London Action Group appeared on the ballot in wards in Camden, Ealing, Kensington and Chelsea, Lewisham, Richmond and Westminster (Craig, 1974; GLC, 1974).

Moreover, given the small size of local government constituencies, especially at second-tier level, it is possible for geographically concentrated interest groups to run a candidate on their own behalf in a particular ward with some hope of his finding support in that ward. Thus on occasions candidates will be put forward by a tenants' association in wards with a high concentration of local authority housing with the aim of defending the interests of council tenants (cf. Brier and Dowse, 1969, for a case study in Exeter). At the Essex County elections of 1973, the leader of the Anti-Maplin Defenders of Essex was elected on a platform of opposition to the proposed Third London Airport by the voters in one of the areas most directly affected by the proposals.

The fact that organisations not normally identified as political parties, and often acting mainly as pressure groups, nominate candidates at local elections and occasionally secure their election means that the hard and fast distinction attempted by Castles for example does not always apply in the context of local politics. This is particularly the case where a local pressure group manages to portray itself as having a wider social base and broader concerns than the particular interests or issues out of which it sprang. In these circumstances, one sees the emergence of what may be described as a genuine local political party (Grant, 1971c).

The issue is further complicated by the fact that, although declining in numbers, Independent local politicians are still encountered, in rural areas especially. It will sometimes be an open question as to how far they do in fact represent the interests of particular pressure groups which have persuaded them to stand for election, or indeed of a particular political party whose views they hold even if they eschew its label.

So far we have identified pressure groups, local political parties, and Independent politicians as actors in the local political system outside the national parties and their branches. There are two more actors characterised basically by their relationship to the national parties. On the one hand are various anti-Socialist caucuses operating under a variety of labels and with a variety of internal composition. On the other hand are splinter parties who on occasion may split away locally from a national party with significant local consequences: the most dramatic example in recent years has been the Democratic Labour Association in Lincoln associated with the former MP Dick Taverne. Finally it is necessary to mention the existence of ratepayers' groups which operate both on the council and amongst local residents. However there is no copyright on the title of ratepayer and such groups may vary widely in their membership and aims as well as in their degree of attachment to the National Union of Ratepayers Associations. In many cases they may be in effect local parties of the type already referred to, or pressure groups, or even anti-Socialist caucuses.

To summarise, in examining local politics beyond the confines of the national parties, we must look at no fewer than five differing actors within the local political system – the Independent, the local party, the splinter party, the anti-Socialist caucus, and the pressure group.[1] Even in making these distinctions it has to be borne in mind that over time, the fortunes, the relationships and the personnel of these bodies can change remarkably since few of them operate, like the national party branches, within any permanent framework transcending time and place and thereby ensuring some form of continuity and consistency despite local vicissitudes.

The Independents

It may be said of the Independent councillor, as of the iceberg, that what is visible is of less significance than that which is hidden from view. The Independent councillor does not necessarily arrive in the council chamber without having gone through some prior process of persuasion and recruitment, followed by electioneering. Nor once elected – or returned unopposed – can he take part in the management of the local authority without entering into some sort of relationship, if not commitment, towards his fellow councillors even if they are all non-party Independents. Thus, in assessing the role of the Independent councillor, we need to pay regard not merely to his personal qualities as an individual, but to the nature and the aims of the 'sponsoring groups' which may have secured his candidacy, and to the means whereby groupings of Independent councillors can hope to influence or control the policy of the council on which they sit.

Unfortunately, the very fact that by virtue of his Independent label, he disclaims any loyalties other than to his conscience makes it singularly difficult for anyone, including the voter, to ascertain what other obligations or sympathies such a councillor may have. Thus for example Grant points out that potential candidates may be sought out, persuaded to stand, and even actively supported by diverse sponsoring groups varying from informal groups of like-minded people to specific bodies such as Rotary or the Chamber of Commerce (Grant, 1973, p.242). The criteria employed by such groups in deciding the merits of a potential councillor are clearly a matter of some consequence, but may not be easily ascertainable by the public. The very nature of the exercise, with its 'soundings-out', its informal procedures and its public disavowal of political commitment make the discovery of these criteria almost impossible. Almost inevitably however, one cannot avoid the implicit assumption that the Independent councillor thus produced, although a creature of uncertain political paternity, has a probable affinity with those sponsors who have adopted him, if their identity can be discovered. By and large these sponsors are prima facie likely to come from those sections of society who are least happy about councillors operating as party politicians, which would in turn suggest that they are unlikely to include many individuals sympathetic to Labour with its firm commitment to party politics.

Indeed some commentators have gone as far as to suggest that many Independent councillors and their sponsors are merely undeclared Conservatives. Thus Johnson, reviewing the elections to the Norfolk County Council from 1946 to 1967 has observed that the number of Conservative candidacies falls when the number of Independent candidacies rises, and vice versa. This he argues suggests 'a rough equivalance between the two categories'. Moreover, in election years when Conservative prospects seemed good, or when Labour opposition

was in prospect, some Independents had sought the security of
Conservative nominations (Johnson, 1972). A similar closeness of
relationship has been observed in Cheshire. In the 1970 County
elections, the Conservatives invited those of their party members who
had been sitting as Independents to accept the Conservative Whip. One
third of the Independents did so or retired to be replaced by
Conservatives. At the same time the previous 'gentleman's agreement'
whereby Conservatives refrained from contesting certain Independent
seats was abandoned (Lee *et al.*, 1974, p.115).

This attempt in Cheshire to make Independents of Conservative
persuasion fight under the party banner merely pre-figured a national
strategy that was to develop in the 1973 local elections. As remarked in
the previous chapter these elections saw a determined attempt by the
Conservatives, with deliberate encouragement from Central Office, to
force Independents to acknowledge their Conservative leanings, or else
face an official Conservative candidate. The decline in the number of
Independent councillors elected in 1973 suggests either that a large
number of Independents adopted a Conservative label or alternatively
that where they refused to do so, the voters preferred to choose
someone whose party allegiance was made clear.

Once elected to a council, Independent members have faced the
problem of how to operate effectively. Sometimes, they have found it
expedient to attach themselves to what becomes known as a
'Conservative and Independent Group' (cf. Jones, 1969, pp.191-3).
Where there has been an Independent 'majority', the task of leadership
has fallen upon individuals, or groups based upon personal qualities,
personal loyalties, seniority or social or geographical interests. Failing
the emergence of some form of Independent leadership the tasks of
co-ordination and of policy formulation must inevitably devolve upon
the chief officers. In either case, whether leadership is exercised by
officers or by various groupings, alliances, or cliques of councillors, it
is hard to see how the Independents can be made collectively
accountable to the electorate since they normally deny any collective
identity. This problem would of course loom even larger in authorities
committed to notions of corporate management and thus to the idea of
infusing the authority with some collective goals. Indeed it may be that
ultimately corporate management and non-party councillors are
mutually incompatible.

The Local Party and the Splinter Party

It seems advisable to consider these two phenomena in conjunction with one another since in practice they may not always be easy to distinguish. This is particularly the case where a local party arises because of dissatisfaction with the way in which one of the established national parties handles a local situation. Under such circumstances disgruntled members of the national party may join others in setting up a new local party which thus reflects in part a fragmentation of one of the established parties.

An essential defining characteristic of these parties is their willingness to contest elections against all comers, rather than against only selected opposition. This differentiates them from the anti-Socialist caucuses with their commitment solely to fighting Labour candidates, and absolves them from the charge of being merely satellites, or disguised versions, of one of the national parties.

Given that these parties arise in response to some local situation it is understandable that attempts to classify them may be hampered by the variety of potential causes of their creation. Grant (1971c) has made a useful attempt at classification, although one of his types – the tenant's party on a council housing estate – arguably straddles the ill-defined boundary between pressure groups and local parties. The distinction between a local party and a local pressure group is hard to make but the party has something to say about the local community as a whole, something which implies outwardly at least a broader concern than with a sectional interest, but which cannot be said from within the confines of a national party branch. The key concern of the true local party is 'what kind of town do we want?' It reflects a concern over a particular community life-style and represents a reaction – often by a particular section of local society – to actual or feared changes to that life-style. Thus the sort of situations in which local parties may be expected to emerge are in small communities suddenly faced with major expansion, seaside towns where tourism threatens the peace and quiet of the residents, and urban areas with a growing immigrant population (cf. Grant, op. cit.) In these situations local parties may emerge committed to resisting the incursions of newcomers, of the commercial holiday trade, or of coloured immigrants in the name of defending the traditional life-style. In so doing such parties will deploy a variety of arguments alleging the inadequacy of amenities in relation to the proposed changes, the inability of the community to absorb the changes, and the undesirable financial implications for existing ratepayers, and asserting the prior claims and interests of existing residents.

Thus in Witham in Essex the acceptance of the town's expansion by both Labour and the Conservatives led to the emergence of an anti-expansion group with close links to the local amenity society. In Torquay in the mid-1960s opposition to spending ratepayers' money on facilities for the holiday trade was expressed briefly by a Residents and Ratepayers' Association who saw the town as a quiet residential haven rather than as a resort (Smith, in Sharpe, 1967). In Bradford the local hostility to coloured immigrants found expression in the Campaign to Stop Immigration which intervened, possibly decisively, in the city elections of 1971 (Bentley, 1972; Richardson & Lethbridge, 1972).

In all these cases the local parties emerged because none of the national parties locally seemed prepared to take up the life-style issues in the manner sought by the dissidents. This contrasts for example with the situation in Ashford, in Kent, where Labour's enthusiasm for expansion was met by hostility from the Conservatives rather than by acquiescence, thus making any separate anti-expansion party unnecessary (Brown *et al.*, 1972). Clearly, where the national parties do not between them articulate any debate on these life-style issues, those who give them pride of place on the local political agenda have little alternative but to form their own local party and to proclaim the irrelevance and impropriety of national party politics on the local scene. In doing so they may draw on activists and electoral support from former adherents of both national parties or of none or primarily from one rather than another. In Witham for example the rise of the anti-expansion group was paralleled by a decline in local Conservative fortunes at the polls and by the election to the Council under the anti-expansion banner of a former Conservative councillor, whilst Labour retained its electoral strength and suffered no significant defections. In Bradford the leading figure in the anti-immigrant group was a former Conservative city councillor, who was credited by the Conservative Leader on the council with siphoning off sufficient Conservative votes to deny the party control of the council in the city elections of 1971 (Bentley, 1972, p.47).

In the latter cases the establishing of a new local party meant some fragmentation of the existing structure of local political support for one of the national parties. Indeed given the strong hold of the national parties in urban areas it is arguable that no local party could ever hope to prosper unless in some way it could subvert the local foundations of one of the national parties. This is why the distinction between local parties and splinter parties is so hard to make.

The most successful recent example of a splinter party has been that of the Democratic Labour Association in Lincoln which grew out of the controversy surrounding the relationship between the Lincoln Labour

Party and the then Labour MP Dick Taverne. The pro-Taverne
Democratic Labour group secured control of the council in 1973 by
calling into question the local political style of the anti-Taverne Labour
Party which had previously controlled the council and by linking this
issue to specific environmental questions regarding the future of
Lincoln (Ramsden and Jay, 1973). A similar, but less successful splinter
party was the Independent Labour Association of Wolverhampton in
the 1930s which split away from its parent party over a dispute
concerning the MP W.J. Brown (Jones, 1969, pp.59-62 and 86-9). It
may be significant that personal loyalties played such a part in these
splits: the same seems to have been true in the cases of the far less
effectual groups in Islington and Basildon in the 1960s and early 1970s,
the New Liberal and the Independent Labour groups respectively.

If we can attempt a distinction between splinter parties and local
parties perhaps it lies along the following lines. Splinter parties emerge
from within the national parties as a result of internal conflicts of
personality, which may be associated with issues of national policy as
in Lincoln. Local parties arise from conflicts within the community as
to the future life-style of the community, conflicts which the national
parties do not articulate. However, if they are to succeed, local parties
may have effectively to capture some of the adherents of a national
party and thus cause it to splinter but from without rather than from
within. It is thus tempting to see these local parties as being in some
ways similar to the nationalist parties of Wales and Scotland in terms of
their impact on the traditional party system.

The Anti-Socialist Caucus

Given the current commitment of the Conservatives to the practice of
contesting local elections under their own party label, together with the
importance of local elections to the Liberals as possible seed-beds for
political development, it seems that the Anti-Socialist Caucus is now
receding into history as an actor on the local political stage. These
caucuses were essentially creatures of the years when Labour was making
its most substantial inroads into local government. Since one of the
complaints against Labour in this situation was its commitment to
party, those who opposed it could scarcely do so by emulating its
example. Thus opposition to growing Labour activity was often
expressed not through local campaigns by the Conservative or Liberal
parties but by the creation of special 'non-party' bodies which could
fight the advance of (Labour) party activity in local politics. These
bodies were not normally based on a mass membership or even on a

permanent organisation. They centred around the group of councillors who were elected under the local anti-Labour banner. They were thus essentially a caucus of local politicians allied in a common hostility to the style and purpose of Labour politics but bound by no commitments to any permanent body of followers. At election time they relied on an *ad hoc* campaign organisation, and were themselves responsible for securing would-be councillors to stand as candidates.

The titles and internal political composition of these caucuses varied widely not merely from one place to another but in the same town from one time to another. Their candidates have appeared under a variety of labels such as Anti-Socialists, Ratepayers, Citizens, Progressives, Municipal Alliance and Moderates. In Sheffield the Citizens' Party founded in 1919 was replaced by the Progressive Party in the 1930s, whilst in Southampton the Independent Party of 1920 became the Ratepayers' Party in 1934 (Hampton, 1970, p.63; Richards, in Sharpe, 1967, p.192). The political composition of such groups as these varied but there seems to have been a consistent predominance of Conservatives within them. Thus the Bristol Citizen Party was formed in 1924 out of a growing co-operation on the council between Conservatives and Liberals. However, from 1947 onwards Liberal candidates appeared on their own behalf and for the next two decades the Citizens became closely identified with the local Conservatives. Leading Citizens were able to hold office in Conservative branches, Conservative agents acted for Citizen Party candidates, and a special Bristol Conservative Association-Citizens Advisory Committee was established (Clements, in Sharpe. 1967, pp.46-8). Similarly the Northumberland Voters' Association was founded in 1947 largely from Conservative and Independent county councillors plus one or two Liberal county councillors (despite its title, the body had no ordinary voter-members). Notwithstanding a certain eclecticism in its willingness to extend membership to any non-Labour councillor the caucus kept in close touch with Conservative constituency officers and advised its own candidates to seek financial help from their local Conservative association in the first instance (Beith, 1973). In Southampton the Ratepayers' Party eventually amalgamated with the local Conservative Party 'from which it had become indistinguishable' (Richards, in Sharpe, 1967, p.192).

In the interwar years the anti-Socialist caucuses may well have represented an attempt at a cross-party alliance of anti-Labour forces from the Conservative, Liberal and Independent camps. In many cases they were partly the result of an ailing Liberal Party seeking refuge

with the Conservatives as Labour began to seize control of former
Liberal wards (Cook, 1975). However, with the passage of time the
caucuses became increasingly to resemble disguised Conservative
caucuses. The decline of the Liberals, especially from the 1930s
onwards, left the Conservatives in a dominating position. After 1945
the growing readiness of Conservatives to fight under the party banner
led to the withering away of the caucuses, sometimes under direct
attack from younger, more partisan, Conservatives (Robbins, 1972).
The highly partisan stance taken by the Conservatives at the 1973
elections for the new authorities now seems to have effectively ended
the heyday of the anti-Socialist caucus, although a few still persist –
for example the Progressives of South Tyneside.

Pressure Groups

The essential characteristic of pressure groups is that their aim is to
influence government. This may not be their sole function but it is one
of their main aims. Moreover, their tactics in doing so normally exclude
entering into electoral contests with the established parties, although
the particular circumstances of local politics may lead to the emergence
of purely localised parties possessing some of the traditionally sectional
or specialised concerns of the pressure group.

Local pressure groups are, broadly, of three types. Some are based
on economic interests such as Trades Councils or Chambers of
Commerce; others on the provision of voluntary services, such as the
Women's Royal Voluntary Service; others on a territorial interest, such
as residents' associations and community groups (Redcliffe-Maud and
Wood, 1974, p.72). In addition there may be sources of pressure which
are not specifically organised into groups such as local industrial firms.
There have been conflicting opinions as to what real influence, if any
pressure groups have achieved in local politics.

Thus some observers have argued that compared with the United
States, Britain exhibits a very low level of local pressure group activity
(Elkin, 1974a, pp.92-113; Banfield and Wilson, 1963, p.246). Similar
comments have been made in the light of research undertaken for the
Maud Committee (CMLG, 1967, vol.4, p.85). This low level of activity
is attributed to the discouragement of participation that stems from a
deferential political culture, and to the disciplined operation of parties
(Elkins, loc. cit.). Other commentators have been less concerned with
comparative questions such as this, and more with the problems of
what local pressure groups do when they are active. In particular they
have raised the issues of whether pressure groups are concerned chiefly

with influencing policy or merely its detailed administration, and
whether they try to channel their views primarily to the councillors or
to the officers.

It does seem reasonable to assume that pressure groups will be
active at those points in the structure of government 'which are most
rewarding in terms of their ability to take the decisions which the
group wants taken' (Moodie and Studdert-Kennedy, 1970, p.74). This
however presupposes that the groups concerned are in fact able to
identify these key points in the local government structure. This in
turn assumes a fairly sophisticated appreciation of whereabouts power
lies in any one local authority. Although constitutionally it may be the
case that pressure over policy issues would be best directed at
councillors and pressure on detailed administration at officers, the
local realities may vary widely. As we have seen, power may lie with
the chief officers, with the Majority Party Group as a whole, with
individual committee chairmen, or with a small group of 'elder
statesmen'. Moreover, given the varying enthusiasms of councillors for
dealing with details as well as with policy, it becomes even harder for
outside groups to determine at which point in the structure to apply
their pressure. In the absence of any clear perception of where the real
power lies, groups may fall back on applying pressure at the most visible
and most accessible point which is most likely to be the elected
councillors for the ward or local authority concerned. Knowledge of
how the local machinery in fact operates will be the key factor in how
groups decide to apply pressure.

Thus the key variables in the behaviour of local pressure groups
become the local balance of power between and amongst councillors
and officers, and the ability of the groups to divine that balance either
through long experience or through inside information. Some groups of
course are well placed to obtain the necessary insights. Many voluntary
service organisations are in frequent contact with the local authority
and learn who best to approach for a particular purpose. Other local
groups have leaders who mix socially with councillors and chief officers
and who can thus sound them out as to appropriate strategies. In brief,
it seems likely that whether concerned with policy or administration,
'insider' groups will approach the right people; 'outsider' groups, newly
formed, unused to dealing with local government, socially distant from
the council, will approach the outward manifestation of authority, the
councillors, who may or may not be the right people to assist them.

Clearly the forms of pressure applied to the right people will differ
from those applied to councillors at large. Correspondence,

word-of-mouth, telephoning, private meetings, rounding up allies and sympathisers, are appropriate means for handling chief officers, committee chairmen and leaders of party Groups. By contrast pressurising the councillors at large may entail circular letters, petitions, demonstrations, press and publicity campaigns, public meetings, and threats to contest elections, as well as behind-the-scenes lobbying of individual councillors and their political parties. Given the contrast here between essentially private and public methods of applying pressure it is not wholly surprising that at present we know rather more about the links between pressure groups and councillors in general than we do about the variety of private contacts between pressure groups and those particular individuals who exert real power in local authorities.

Unlike MPs, councillors have to live and conduct their politics in close proximity to those whom they serve. They are thus more immediately accessible to pressure groups; one pressure group organiser goes so far as to suggest that they are also thereby more amenable to pressure than are such remote figures as Ministers, MPs and civil servants (Hall, 1974, p.72). However, mere geographical availability is hardly likely to be the sole factor in determining how receptive a councillor is to the application of pressure. Elkin suggests that councillors may have a unitary view of the public interest, which predisposes them to search for some general good, rather than to try and accommodate various conflicting interests through an American-style politics of bargaining (Elkin, 1974a, p.124). Even where the reality of conflicting interests is acknowledged, the councillors may nevertheless regard themselves as constituting an adequate cross-section of the public at large, embracing a variety of interests and thus able to resolve conflicts amongst themselves without any need for outside consultation (Maddick and Pritchard, 1959, p.140). Thus it is by no means certain that the councillors' availability will automatically be translated into a welcome and encouragement to pressure group activity. Much is likely to depend on the criteria by which councillors judge individual pressure groups and their actions.

Dearlove suggests that councillors' judgements about pressure groups will be made on the basis of the character of the group, the nature of its demand and the method of communicating the demand (Dearlove, 1973, p.157). Certain types of group may readily display the right character. For example voluntary organisations supplementing the social services, or local amenity societies whose style of approach to councillors is seen as 'helpful' to them may be approved by those councillors. These groups are seen as positive, established and respectable. Moreover, they may be as much concerned with helping the council to achieve its aims as with importuning for provisions which the council cannot make. They are thus giving the council as much, sometimes more, than they themselves gain. Of course, in particular localities other groups may have no difficulty in acquiring a good character reference. In strong Labour areas the local Trades Council may have ready access to the councillor's ear; in Conservative authorities local commerce and industry may be similarly well-placed. Much may depend on whether or not local councillors are themselves involved in a particular organisation. Councillors belong to more local organisations than the average citizen (CMLG, 1967, vol.2, p.184), and their links — active or honorific — with such bodies are likely to provide those bodies with the stamp of good character.

Turning to the nature of the demands made by pressure groups, a basic issue will be whether or not the demand is within the competence of the authority. Some demands may be beyond the council's ability to fulfill simply because in ignorance they are addressed to the wrong authority, or because the pattern of existing commitments such as a capital works programme cannot be changed. If a demand could in principle be met then the key questions are whether it is in line with the council's image of what it ought to do in fulfilling its role, and whether there are already other competing demands against which it may have to be judged. Here we come up against the councillor's predisposition to favour certain groups or levels of service in the community which of course derives from his own social and political background.

As to the methods by which the demands are conveyed to councillors it seems to be the case that the more aggressive, or flamboyant, or publicity-conscious the method, the less acceptable the councillors find it. Thus such techniques as petitions, using the local Press, holding demonstrations, or applying pressure from some national headquarters (if a local group has one) are all frowned upon, with preference being given to direct contact with the individual councillors most concerned, such as the ward member or the committee chairman (Dearlove, 1973, pp.161-2; Cousins, 1973b, p.23).

The character of a group, its demands, and its methods of communication are likely to be closely linked. An unorthodox radical group may make unorthodox and radical demands, with unorthodox and radical methods of communication. Indeed some form of cumulative causation may set in whereby initial failure to get demands acceded to, may encourage more aggressive tactics leading to a worsening of the image of the group's character in the eyes of councillors. Conversely, approved groups making approved demands will not need to use disapproved tactics.

In the last analysis councillors are likely to view a pressure group, its character, its demands and its methods as a simple package. Their judgement of it will reflect not merely the overall impression they have of the group itself, but also the notions they have of the proper duties and responsibilities of local government and the most desirable style of local politics. It is these which are the yardsticks by which councillors will measure the acceptability of pressure groups and their demands. They are yardsticks which, in their construction, owe much to the social and political background of the councillors.

From the councillor's point of view perhaps the main merit of pressure groups is that they provide him with information and with arguments which may have been ignored or distorted by the official machinery of the local authority. The utility of such groups in presenting such organised opinion and information has been acknowledged by councillors in both Sheffield and Birmingham although this is not to say that they are always swayed by the representations made (Hampton, 1970, pp.71 and 217; Newton, 1974b, p.628). Some groups can of course also claim the special merit that they are not merely making demands from time to time, but are providing a local service which it might otherwise fall upon the council to provide. Councillors are much in favour of such bodies meeting local needs, especially in new or developing fields, perhaps with assistance from the council (CMLG, 1967, vol.2, pp.191-2). Although they would thus find councillors favourably disposed towards them such organisations do in fact prefer dealing with officers rather than with members (Cousins, 1973b, p.21; Newton, 1973, p.299). Indeed, their contact with officers may not even be at chief officer level but at second and third tier level (Cousins, loc. cit.). Their apparent preference for this form of contact suggests that such organisations know both what they want and who to ask and they may thus be classic examples of the 'insider' groups mentioned previously.

In talking of the councillor − pressure group relationship, we have abstracted the councillors from the party political context within which many of them work. To do so is of course to obscure the fact that one way of trying to influence politicians is through the party to which they owe allegiance. This may be especially relevant at the level of local government, where policy decisions can be taken by the entire party Group on the council, as compared with the Cabinet at national level. Thus party pressure even on the most humble back-bencher may be of some use at local level in trying to obtain a favourable decision.

Attempts at influencing a party may be direct or indirect. In the latter case, the essential ingredient is to persuade a party that there is some special political benefit to be gained from adopting a given line of policy. Thus the London Motorway Action Group and its allies, with articulate spokesmen concentrated in a small number of marginal constituencies, were able to persuade Labour that there was an electoral advantage in, as well as environmental justification for, abandoning the GLC ringway proposals. Attempts at directly influencing a party can only succeed if the issue can be plausibly presented in the ideological language of the party concerned. This presupposes some degree of familiarity and contact between pressure group and party. In practice, parties and certain pressure groups are likely to have close links, social and personal if not formal, which provide useful channels for campaigning for a particular cause. Thus Trades Councils may well have close links with the local Labour Party whilst bodies such as Rotary and the Chamber of Commerce may have ready entry to Conservative circles. On the issue of comprehensive education, the links between local teachers, the Socialist Education Association, the Confederation for the Advancement of State Education, and local Labour parties have provided very effective channels of communication and of lobbying (Hampton, 1970, pp.236-7; Peterson, 1971, p.397). Conversely, in Hull, the mainly middle-class advocates of fluoridation had little access to the Hull Labour Party and its council Group, who rejected the scheme (Brier, 1970, p.162).

Clearly, use of the parties as a vehicle for pressurising councils depends on having adequate access to them and on not raising issues that run counter to their general outlook. Even if these conditions are met however, there is no guarantee that the party organisation can command the votes of its councillors in the chamber. Nevertheless, for certain groups in the community, given the overlap in interest and in membership between themselves, the parties and the respective party Groups, it makes sense to use these links if only to maintain a general state of mutual benevolence. In this sense the parties can serve to aggregate some of the interests in the community if not all of them. Smallwood (1965, p.156) and Bealey and his colleagues (1965, p.380) all emphasise the ability of groups to work through parties rather than run independent campaigns: this may owe much to the closer correspondence of the class bases of the parties and of some pressure groups in Britain compared with the United States (Newton, 1969, p.213).

Despite the very rapid expansion in local presssure group activity during and since the 1960s, it cannot be said that the pressure group world encompasses the entire population of a community. Even on the basis of a fairly generous definition of local organisations, some 39 per cent of the electorate are non-joiners, and of the remaining 61 per cent who are members, two-thirds are purely nominal members who take no active part in any organisation. Moreover, membership in local organisations is more likely to be found amongst the better educated in the community (CMLG, 1967, vol.III, tables 159 and 167). Amongst the voluntary welfare groups for example, active members are 'more likely to come from the upper occupational groups, and to be better educated, and probably better off, than the average citizen' (Aves, 1969, para.38). In Birmingham, Newton found that the secretaries of local organisations were middle or upper class, and that there was a good deal of overlap between office holders in the various bodies (Newton, 1974a, p.6). In terms of its active personnel and its style of operation, if not in its interests and assumptions, the local group system is thus largely the domain of a middle-class minority. In that sense it is clearly a loaded and an unbalanced system. For those active within it it certainly provides a refuge for those who find the machinations of local party politics distasteful, yet still seek to exert some influence in local affairs. It also provides a local mechanism of social integration for, and amongst, the socially and geographically mobile middle class. 'To the working-class, life in the village means family life and possibly life at work; to the middle-class spiralists, life in the village means life in the voluntary associations.' (Pahl, 1970, p.66.)

As well as being socially unrepresentative the world of local pressure groups is not entirely comprehensive in terms of the issues and attitudes it embraces. Not all points of view will be equally represented. There are for example few anti-amenity groups although a concern for good visual standards in public places is by no means universal. The prospects for equality amongst pressure groups are made further remote by the great disparity which exists amongst groups in terms of their membership, their income, their staff and other resources. The existence of pressure groups, and of the other political actors considered in this chapter does allow some variety in the local political debate. It introduces individuals, and ways of looking at local problems, which are neither of them constrained by the requirements of formal loyalty to a national political party. There is not of course a total divorce between the two forms of local politics. Party members are more likely to be members of non-party voluntary associations than are other citizens:

indeed, the more active the member is in his party the more likely he is to be active in other associations (Berry, 1970, pp.53-60). Nevertheless it is true that the various groups and individuals which engage in local politics outside the ranks of the national political parties do represent a modest widening and enrichment of the area of debate. They do not however provide avenues whereby the bulk of the population participate in the process of influencing and taking decisions.

Notes

1. In Scotland and Wales of course the Scottish National Party and Plaid Cymru might be added to the list: they are however national rather than local parties in the overall context of Scottish and Welsh politics.

5 THE COUNCIL AND THE PEOPLE

Local authorities, through the services they provide, impinge directly or indirectly on the lives of most of their citizens. Nevertheless, their impact is one which most people take for granted and which may not be easily distinguished in their own minds from the role played in their lives by other public bodies such as the health service, the employment exchange or the post office. Knowledge of and interest in local government, which are themselves prior requirements for taking part in local politics, are perhaps best described as generally rudimentary for the majority of the population. Thus the Maud Committee found that one in five of the electorate were unable to name any of the services which were provided by their local authorities, even though 98 per cent of them were aware of receiving at least one service which, did they but know it, was provided by the council (CMLG, 1967, vol.3, tables 2 and 58). The problem thus seems to be one of lack of awareness of the allocation of responsibilities. This seemed to be more especially the case in areas with two-tier local government, in contrast to county boroughs (CMLG, 1967, vol.3, p.7). The extension of two-tier government to the entire country (apart from the Scottish Islands), and the re-shuffling of responsibilities between the tiers, thus seems unlikely to have improved public comprehension of which authorities provide what service.

As for their degree of interest in the work of their local council, some 65 per cent of those interviewed for the Kilbrandon Commission claimed to be 'quite interested' or 'very interested', compared with 81 per cent with the same degrees of interest in central government (RCC, 1973, Research Paper 7, Table 4).[1] This does not of course enable us to gauge the nature of their interest, nor the aspects of the council's work which most attracts their attention. Given the somewhat low turnout at local elections, however, it seems reasonable to suggest that their interest is in local authorities as providers of services, rather than as instruments of democracy in action.

In terms of direct contacts with local government just under one person in five has seen or been in touch with a councillor at some time or other, and just over one in four with a council officer (RCC, op. cit., table 5). Few people have ever attended a meeting of their local council, and there is some evidence that even the proportion of 7 per cent who claim to have done so may be an overestimate (CMLG, 1967, vol.3, table 83, and vol.5, pp.421 and 422).

Clearly the attitude of the public to local government must partly reflect the extent of their knowledge and contacts with it, and also the outcome of their contacts. Contacts, of course, may be made for a variety of reasons, from seeking our information to launching an angry complaint. Not surprisingly the average citizen is easier to satisfy when seeking information than when raising a complaint and requesting that it be remedied. Amongst the small minority of citizens who do refer their grievances to the council over a half (54 per cent) proclaim themselves dissatisfied with the way the complaint was handled — a higher proportion than is the case in relation to large firms, the health service, the central government, or the gas and electricity boards (RCC, 1973, Research Paper 7, table 25). In fact this group of unsatisfied complainants represents only a small minority of the total population, most of whom do not complain at all. The general lack of complaints could of course represent little more than an absence of the energy, self-confidence or knowledge necessary to confront authority. However, the evidence seems to suggest that on the whole most people are not harbouring silent grievances about the way their council functions. The Maud Committee found that 90 per cent of those surveyed thought their district or borough council was 'fairly well' or 'very well' run; 75 per cent had the same opinion of their county council.[2] (CMLG, 1967, vol.3, table 91). Findings for the Kilbrandon Commission indicated that compared with civil servants council officials were regarded as being less efficient, but better at understanding the needs of 'the ordinary man' and better at keeping the public informed about decisions which have been made (RCC, 1973, Research Paper 7, table 29).

Attitudes towards local government may clearly be influenced by the extent to which electors feel that they could influence their council if necessary, or even do the job of a councillor better than the present incumbents. Rather less than half those interviewed for the Maud Commission felt that they might intervene with some hope of success if their council was doing something with which they disagreed, but just over two-thirds of the Kilbrandon respondents felt that existing councillors did a better job than they themselves could do (CMLG, 1967, vol.3, table 105; RCC, 1973, Research Paper 7, table 14). There seems to co-exist a general desire that 'ordinary people' should stand a better chance of getting on the council and a fear that council business may nevertheless be a bit too complicated for the average person to

understand (RCC, op. cit., tables 14 and 17). The latter fear echoes the
'lack of confidence in their ability to do the (councillor's) job' noted by
the Maud Committee (CMLG, 1967, vol.3, p.122).

The constellation of knowledge, interest and attitude towards local
government held by the average citizen can perhaps be best summed up
as one of a rather vague and generalised knowledge, a lukewarm and
rather utilitarian interest, and a modest degree of satisfaction with
performance coupled with doubts as to whether he himself could do
much better in any case. A generalisation such as this, however, does
obscure the important fact that knowledge, interest and attitudes are
not identical throughout the social spectrum. Knowledge of what local
government does is greater amongst men than women, among the
young rather than the old and amongst those with more formal
education. These more knowledgeable groups are more likely to contact
the council office or a local councillor and to feel that they could
influence decisions of the local council. (CMLG, 1967, vol.3, tables
3, 4, 17, 64, 65, 66, 74, 75, 76, 106, 107, 108; RCLGS 1969,
Research Study 2, Section C; RCLGE, 1969, Research Study 9).[3] A
link has also been identified between satisfaction with local authority
services and high social status (RCLGE, op. cit., p.88); this may reflect
the ability of the middle-class resident to defend his interests to his
social peers amongst the councillors and officers. There is here a major
problem for local government, and one which goes some way towards
accounting for the growth of militant community groups in some inner
urban areas: by and large those who are in most contact with local
authorities and whose needs are apparently most readily satisfied tend
to be the better-off sections of the community. Those who have the
worst problems are not in this happy position, but they may of course
entertain lower expectations of seeing their problems solved and thus
rarely express any dissatisfaction.

Members, Officers and the Public

In so far as there is contact, albeit it partial and intermittent between
the citizen and his local council it takes the form of meetings — small
or large, formal or informal — between the citizenry and the councillors
and officers. For many individual residents contact of this type is their
sole means of experiencing the council other than as a remote
bureaucratic machine.

Harrison and Norton found 'very little indication that members
(councillors) play a significant role in supplying information about the
council and its policies to the public in their locality' (CMLG, 1967,

vol.5, p.27). Moreover in voicing their own complaints or making their own enquiries the public prefer, in the first instance at least, to deal with officers rather than with councillors. Indeed, a minority would not consider approaching their councillor at all even as a second or last resort, either because of not knowing who he is or how to contact him or else because of doubts as to whether he can really help (RCLGE, 1969, Research Study 9; RCLGS, 1969, Research Study 2, Section D). Some councillors, though, clearly are approached, for some of them spend several hours a week dealing with individual problems of their constituents (CMLG, 1967, vol.2, tables 8.10 and 8.11). Moreover, there is evidence that the councillors themselves do derive satisfaction from sorting out peoples' personal problems (ibid., table 4.2; Heclo, 1969, p.192). It may be that the electors see this as a more important task for the councillor than general policy making. Buxton argues that in so far as there are pressures on the councillors they are mainly to secure the redress of individual grievances or to oil the wheels of the council machinery, rather than to amend major policies (Buxton, 1973, p.34).

The accessibility of councillors to their constituents depends on a number of factors. For example not all councillors live in the wards they represent. This may be particularly true of some of the poorer working-class wards in inner city areas where councillors may have been imported from suburban areas with a surplus of political talent (Muchnik, 1970, p.106). There are of course a variety of ways of establishing mutual contact, by telephone, by letter, at casual meetings in the street or at work, through advice bureaux or party meetings or voluntary organisations, whilst canvassing at election time, or simply by turning up on the doorstep. Labour councillors seem more likely to work through the ward party meetings, through advice bureaux or by receiving visits at home, whilst Conservatives rely more on correspondence or voluntary organisations as a means of establishing contact with the electors (Newton, 1973 and 1974b; Hampton, 1970, pp.198-201; Dearlove, 1973, p.184). When concerned with sounding out opinion on policies rather than with solving private problems, then party sources become particularly important for councillors, especially on the Labour side (Newton, 1973, pp.292-4). This tendency to consult with political colleagues, especially within the council Group, and to a lesser degree with officers of the local authority, over policy questions rather than with the public at large may be related to the tendency for councillors 'to agree more than electors over most issues' (Budge *et al.*, 1972, p.211). The accessibility of councillors to the public will vary according to their place of residence, their party affiliations and also the degree to which they become embroiled in the statesman's role of making rather than checking decisions. It may, however, be the case that a general climate of accessibility will exist within any one authority. Thus in Cardiganshire, Madgwick found that the small size of the electorate greatly facilitated what he called the intermediary role of the councillor, even to the point where canvassing for council jobs was not unknown (Madgwick, 1973, pp.187-8). Harrison and Norton observed that:

> In general the degree of contact between councillor and public seemed a fairly direct reflection of the normal contacts maintained by citizen with citizen in the district to which the councillor belonged. In a small, close-knit, community where it was said that everyone knew everyone else's business, the pressure on a councillor could be intense. (CMLG, 1967, vol.5, p.25.)

The creation of larger authorities, with larger electorates per councillor, seems likely to weaken the sort of close-knit link between the councillor and his electorate in those areas where it has existed hitherto.

In practice, as we have seen, the electors are rather more likely to deal with officers than with elected members when they come into contact with the council. However, whereas in theory all councillors are, by virtue of their constitutional role, liable to be approached by the public at any time, the same cannot be said of local government officers. Some officers work in positions which entail virtually no public contact — draughtsmen, committee clerks, site engineers, and personnel officers for example. Others may have dealings with the public in an over-the-counter manner akin to that of the shop assistant, for example the library assistant or the cashier, or in some pastoral fashion, such as home-helps and social workers. Heads of department and other senior officers may deal with the public but in a formalised fashion, through organised groups or at special public meetings. When it comes to day-to-day enquiries and complaints, however, it is true to say that most of the contacts are concentrated on a few areas of the council's work, namely council housing, town planning, utility services (e.g. street lights and refuse collection) and to a lesser degree education and welfare (CMLG, 1967, vol.3, tables 70, 71 and 81; RCLGS, 1969, Research Study 2, table 26). Thus for the majority of citizens raising a matter at the town hall the contact is likely to be with an officer of one of the departments dealing with these issues, an officer probably of junior to middling rank, familiar enough with both existing policy and specific situations to be able to deal with the points made by the enquirer or complainant.

Those officers who do come into contact with the public — in whatever manner — seem to find the experience generally satisfactory (CMLG, 1967, vol.3, table 62). Amongst those citizens who take complaints specifically to the officers some 47 per cent proclaim themselves to be in some degree unsatisfied with the way in which the matter is then handled (RCC, 1973, Research Paper 7, table 21). This is not wholly surprising since over time the complaints or requests of various individual citizens may be virtually contradictory or incompatible so that somebody has to be disappointed. Moreover, there is a tendency for officers and the public to see individual problems in a different light. For the citizen his particular problem looms very large and he wants it solved: if it is not to be solved then at least he wants signs of action; and failing action some evidence of interest, sympathy and understanding. In other words the citizen is seeking some form of active and expressive reaction from the officer in terms of a visible outward commitment to deal with the problem. From the point of view of the officer, however, the situation is rather different. Any one case is only one among many, and cases as a whole may be merely but a part of his overall workload. His reaction, far from being active and expressive, is likely to be, initially at least, dominated by questions such as what exactly is the nature of the complaint, how does it arise, what are the correct channels, have they all been used up, are there precedents, is there a policy, are there insuperable obstacles, and (often most important of all) do I really understand the whole story behind this particular complaint? Answering all these questions of course can take time, and require all manner of consultation with other officers and other departments. Thus it is hardly surprising that the reaction of the officer to a complaining citizen combines caution in equal proportion to his concern and thus precludes the appearance of immediate signs of remedying the wrong which has sparked off the complaint.

So far we have considered the relationship between the citizen and his council in terms essentially of the citizen as consumer of the services which the council provides, rather than as an active participant, through a democratic process, in their provision as well as their consumption. Even if we see the citizen as a mere consumer, and still more so if he is regarded as an active participant in relation to local government, there must ideally be some other means of communication between citizen and council, and vice versa, over and above the individual contacts

enjoyed by a minority of the electorate from time to time. The greater
the flow of information and opinion between government and governed
the better the government: that is the traditional supposition of liberal
representative democracy. There may of course be more radical
democratic mechanisms with potential for linking and indeed blending
governors and governed such as the various tactics of community
politics and public participation. Traditionally, however, local
government has relied on the media and on elections as the main means
of communication between the council and the citizen.

Local Politics and the Media

Reference has already been made to the fact that councillors do not
play a significant part in keeping their constituents informed about the
council and its policies. The claim has been made that it is not the
councillor but the local press which is 'the link between electors and
elected' (Benham, 1964, p.251). In the field of planning one journalist
argues that:

> . . .the local press is the chief means of communication between a
> planning committee and the public for whom it is supposed to be
> planning. . .the local newspaper is virtually the only forum in which
> considered discussion of local planning issues can take place.
> (Jenkins, 1973a, p.50.)

These claims gain some support from findings in Glasgow that 'the vast
majority of electors, even for local matters, still rely upon the mass
media for most of their information', with little evidence of
communications flowing from councillors, through party workers, to
electors (Budge *et al.,* 1972, p.142).

Certainly the great majority of electors (four out of five) are regular
readers of local newspapers, including both weeklies and provincial and
London evening dailies. Local weeklies are the more often read, and of
course the most widely available. Moreover, the local press is the most
frequently cited source amongst the third of the electorate who claim
to have heard recent news of local council activity (CMLG, 1967, vol.3,
Tables 32, 36, 38, 40; RCLGS, 1969, Research Study 2, p.22). The
local press is thus indeed an important source of council news for a
minority of the population, far more so than the councillors or the
officers. Even so it does not seem to penetrate as far into every corner
of the electorate as the more optimistic press-men might like to
believe.

Given, nevertheless, that it does perform a modestly useful role in linking the council and the electorate, the question must arise as to the type of news and information which the local press conveys and also the municipal values and images which it imparts to its readership. Apart from its important role as an advertiser of jobs, services, goods, houses, entertainments and the like, the local press can make three contributions to the political life of the community — provide and interpret information, promote a sense of community identity, and act as a platform for debate and complaint (Jackson, 1971, p.279).

An examination of six Merseyside local papers (weekly and daily) in the 1960s found that between 20 and 25 per cent of the papers column inches were devoted to news, as distinct from features, sport and advertising. Of that proportion between a quarter and a half were devoted to news of local government and politics, including local election campaigns, and party meetings and social events. The main individual local government services to receive a mention were education, housing and planning, followed by highways, police and transport (Cox and Morgan, 1973, pp.55-7 and 66). The news items tended to be presented in a somewhat raw fashion, with little attempt to interpret them or to fit them into any wider background of council policy or of the development of the community as a whole.

This is despite the fact that editorially local papers are very sensitive to the need to identify and sustain an image for their community against which both passing events and specific proposals can be judged. The type of image, and thus the type of community, which the press likes to present to its readers is essentially one of a united, prosperous place, not rent by social or political divisions. The main political goal locally is seen to be 'the promotion of the "good of the town", but only occasionally (are) we offered even a vague definition of what this consisted of. It included truths held to be self-evident' (ibid., p.98). The social conservatism of this stance is a common feature of much of the local press which is firmly committed to defence of the family, discipline, tradition and convention, and the Protestant ethic. Weeklies in particular are keen to place their emphasis on these elements of life reflecting harmony and order rather than conflict and disorder (Jackson, 1971, pp.87 and 278).

From observing this set of attitudes it is all too easy to infer that the local press is not merely conservative in its social values but Conservative in its party politics. This does seem to be true of the London and provincial evening dailies to some degree but less so of the weeklies (Jackson, 1971, pp.266-8). However, this non-partisanship at the level of the local weeklies may be a largely post-1945 development. Before that date in the suburbs at least, 'the local press may have provided a strong right-wing influence' (Todd, 1975, p.286). It could be the case that the right-wing partisanship which Todd has observed reflected hostility to the incursion of Labour into local politics between the wars. The local press after 1945 may have come to an accommodation with the new reality of local party politics, and have decided that further continued partisanship was now both politically pointless and bad for business.

If the local government news which the press reports is rather undigested, and if the image of the local community which it imparts is somewhat bland, what of the role of the local paper as a forum for debate and complaint? The main vehicles available for this are the editorials and the correspondence columns. We know little about the total size and contents of an editor's post-bag, although Jenkins noted that local environmental issues formed the single biggest topic of letter writers to the London *Evening Standard* (Jenkins, 1973a, p.49). From his own study, Jackson found that the local government image that dominates the correspondence columns is one of 'a sphere of officialdom (containing) latent autocratic or pompous attitudes ever ready to erupt. . .lacking a proper sense of priorities so that its decisions. . .may well be misguided if not downright wrong' (Jackson, 1971, p.161). This tone of antagonism towards the local council is in one sense encouraged by the editors who '. . .evidently prefer correspondents to shoulder much of the burden of direct, uncompromising criticism of the council, whereas editorials, even when sounding a warning note to the council, are generally restrained and circumspect in tone' (ibid., pp.275-6).

The willingness of the press to let its readers shoulder the burden of local criticism of authority has to be seen against the background of the extent to which the editors and reporters are dependent on the local council for information. Thus journalists concerned with the government of London 'find ourselves telephoning, lunching with, meeting casually and generally coming into contact with permanent local government officials, possibly four or five times as often as with elected councillors' (Jenkins, 1973a, p.52). Similarly, in Merseyside senior officers and councillors were the main source for council news (Cox and Morgan, 1973, p.43). Moreover, some papers may attach great importance to the opinion in which they are held by local community leaders (Jackson, 1971, p.275) and thus will strive to ensure that they present a 'responsible' and 'constructive' tone in their comments on council actions.

The dependence of the press on the council as a news source militates against reporting in a fashion which might imperil the source, and over time the exposure of journalists to the official point of view may produce an unconscious bias towards that perspective on local problems. In simple terms local officials, local politicians and local journalists have to live with one another and to some degree, off one another, and this militates against excessively critical or investigative reporting.

In Glasgow, Budge and his colleagues noted that 'councillors enjoy substantial freedom in emphasising some issues and playing down others. . .(This) seems dependent on (press) correspondents' co-operation. But since the views and interests of the two sides converge the councillor's dependence is not a serious limitation on their freedom of collective action' (Budge *et al.,* 1972, p.238). All in all, it is hardly surprising that most exposures of local government scandals have usually been the work of outsiders from the national press untrammelled by any local obligations or loyalties.

The symbiotic nature of the local press-local authority relationship, is not the sole factor determining the nature of council reporting. There are certain practical constraints to which the press is subject. Despite the increasing grip of the London-based newspaper groups on the provincial dailies nearly half of the evening newspapers and three-quarters of the weeklies are still owned by regional or local proprietors. The circulation and resources of many of these papers are not such as to support a large reporting staff and certainly not large enough to sustain specialist staff in local government or for that matter proper legal advice if investigative journalism were to start entering sensitive areas. With many of their reporters merely serving out an apprenticeship before moving on into the wider world of journalism such papers can rarely expect their staff to acquire any long experience of local government work. For such junior reporters, and hard-pressed editors, the official hand-out, the committee minutes, or a good 'quote' offered by a publicity seeking councillor or an outraged ratepayer are manna from heaven. They can provide a surprise story and a headline, but the prospects of digging behind the handout or the minutes or the quote for some background analysis are minimal. The resources are not there.

Nor is the interest always there. The editors on Merseyside tended to regard local government reporting as a matter of civic duty rather than of choice (Cox and Morgan, 1973, p.122). On the whole journalists' news values do not place a high premium on explicitly political subjects, unless they can be constructed in terms of a clash of personalities, or as sudden upsets in the *status quo* (Tunstall, 1970, p.15; Seymour-Ure, 1974, p.18). In local politics neither the subject matter nor the individuals lend themselves to this treatment very often. Only occasionally does a local politician with a flair for understanding the journalists' preoccupations succeed in dramatising and popularising local government. Herbert Morrison was one such politician (Donoughue and Jones, 1973, pp.207-8): as also, before his fall, was T. Dan Smith.

In any case, local newspapers are a commercial venture and much depends on the relevance of local government to their readership. Circulation areas may bear little relation to local government boundaries. With larger authorities and a universal two-tier structure, many newspapers will find themselves publishing in a town miles away from the new seats of power. For any one paper only a portion of a County or Scottish Regional Council's business will now be relevant. This was always a problem with the county councils, the adequacy of whose reporting often seemed to decline with distance from the county town. A similar pattern could now also occur with the larger Districts.

It is of course true that one consequence of the 1972 Local Government Act and of the 1973 Local Government (Scotland) Act was to widen slightly the access of press and public to committees, though not sub-committees, of the council. Moreover, an increasing number of authorities have appointed officers to deal with public and press relations and have adopted the practice of holding press conferences. It has been argued that on the whole press coverage of committee meetings is the most fruitful source of information to the public about council business, with innovations such as public relations, press conferences and official publications being less important (Taras, 1972). However, in the absence of any tradition of local investigative reporting, the initiative in creating information still lies with the council whatever methods it employs to convey it to press and public. Councillors can always meet privately to discuss business outside of formal committee meetings. Party group meetings are important points of decision taking but are invariably in private, although in Sunderland the Labour Group opened its meetings to the press without undue disaster. The initiative in formulating and publicising the agenda of local politics lies with the council. At national level it may be the case that, as Lord Boyle claims, 'The Cabinet increasingly, as the years go on, tends to be most concerned with the agenda that the press and media are setting out as the crucial issues before the nation at any one time.' (Boyle and Crosland, 1971, p.109.) But this is certainly not true locally.

There is no local equivalent of the parliamentary lobby, and it is certainly hard to conceive of a local editor with the political influence of, say, Geoffrey Dawson of *The Times,* with his network of contacts and correspondence (Seymour-Ure, 1974, pp.86-7). Indeed when local politicians complain about the local press, as they do from time to time, their complaints are not akin to Baldwin's notorious accusation of 'power without responsibility'. Rather do they complain about misinterpretation, trivialisation, inadequate analysis, absence of perspective and a general lack of sustained interest in the ongoing business of the authority until some crisis suddenly arises to produce a headline.

For the average councillors and local government officer, the local press is a source of occasional irritation but almost never a threat. It generally endorses their right to make decisions, even if they make the occasional bad one; it presents a bland and not overly informative picture of local government, its commitment to the notion of 'the good of the town' and to the idea of order and harmony prevent it from analysing or exploiting sectional disagreements and grievances; and its lack of resources prevent it from developing analytical and investigatory journalism. If the local press is a public watchdog on the town hall it is a singularly accommodating animal, with no bite and a rather muffled bark.

This may help to explain the rise in recent years of a local alternative press with a much more iconoclastic and aggressive stance towards local officials and politicians. Originating in the late 1960s these local community papers now probably number over one hundred, often catering for a quite small circulation area such as a neighbourhood or an estate. Some grew out of a specific local situation or reaction to a particular issue, others were launched by local groups such as a tenants' association, community workers, or radical socialist groups. Whereas the traditional local paper is on the whole a paper of record and a medium of entertainment, the alternative community press is a vehicle for investigation, advice, campaigning and action. They carry stories which the traditional papers ignore; they are quite happy to name their enemies, be they landlords, politicians, officials, local industrialists or whomsoever; they advise on how to establish rights and entitlements *vis-à-vis* public bodies; they campaign on behalf of tenants against landlords, squatters against the council, residents against the developers. Some are given away, some hawked in the streets, some sold by sympathetic shopkeepers. The attitude towards them of the local council varies from giving a council grant in a few cases, through 'tight-lipped suspicion', to being allegedly 'completely demoralised' by them (Ensor, 1975; *Community Action,* Apr.-May, 1974, pp.29-32). As yet they are too few in number to have had more than a purely local impact, but their very existence serves to underline the social conservatism and general timidity of the established press.

The local press — established or alternative — is not the only local mass medium of information. The growth of local radio has opened another means of communication between councils and their communities. Certainly one of the aims of local broadcasting as laid down in the 1966 White Paper was that of 'fostering a greater awareness of local affairs and involvement in the community'. By 1975, there were 20 BBC local radio stations, together with another 19 operating under the IBA. The typical BBC station for example serves between 500,000 and a million people, employs some 20 people, and originates an average of just under 10 hours of programmes a day, plus network material, with an emphasis on news and information (Robertson, 1974 pp.16-17).

In covering local government radio has some problems similar to those of the press. With a small staff and a tight budget, it is often hard to devote adequate time to reporting or mastering any one topic. Although most local stations have a reporter who covers local government as one of his tasks only two have specialised reporters on the subject, namely BBC Radio London and London Broadcasting. There is some significance in the fact that the only two such reporters are based at the GLC. As the largest local authority in the country the GLC generates a great deal of information, its senior politicians are normally at County Hall during the day and are thus accessible to the reporters, and most of the councillors are very articulate and are good radio material (Eccles Interview). It is doubtful whether many other authorities could sustain a full-time reporter by the light of these criteria. Indeed with two radio reporters and two London evening press reporters the GLC is probably the only local authority with its own equivalent of the parliamentary lobby correspondents.

Local politics in London, taking together the GLC and the London Boroughs, can support on one local station — BBC Radio London — a weekly phone-in on local government, news items, interviews, and 'GLC Question Hour' broadcast from the council chamber every three weeks. Audience research in local radio is very inadequate but one estimate is that Radio London has perhaps 700,000 listeners in all (Redhouse Interview). Clearly at that audience level even in Greater London, radio is not yet a major link in the council-citizen chain of communication.

This is due more to the general low level of public listening to local radio than to any hostility by the local authorities towards radio as a medium. Most local stations have a permanent line to, and some sort of studio facilities at, their major local authority headquarters, and live or recorded extracts from council debates have been broadcast in Manchester, Merseyside, Stoke and Leicester as well as from the GLC. However, given the demand on their resources, it usually requires a major debate on a sensitive local issue to make such broadcasts worth while from the point of view of the local station.

Those engaged in local government work vary in their willingness to become involved with local radio. The councillors are often only too willing to appear in interview and discussion programmes, though it is not always the case that those who appear are those with most to contribute. Good committee chairmen are not always good radio material. Officers are rather more wary of radio, especially if they feel there is any danger of making some irretrievable blunder whilst on the air. On the other hand recording and editing is equally likely to provoke claims of misrepresentation both by officers and councillors.

One issue yet to be determined is how far local radio may alter the workings of local government, even if only in minor ways. It is arguable for example that the GLC changed its standing orders on members' question time as a direct result of the unfortunate showing of one committee chairman at a live broadcast of 'Question Hour'. The irretrievable nature of the content of a live broadcast may encourage party groups to plan debates even more carefully, to ensure that no splits or dissensions are apparent to the public. The combined attentions of both local radio and local press may encourage yet more authorities to appoint press officers. This may have the side effect of reducing the direct, and informative, contacts reporters previously enjoyed with chief officers, if not with councillors.

Within the community at large one function which local radio can perform is that of enabling local pressure groups to air their views, although not every locality contains enough groups capable of sustaining a regular series of platform-type programmes. It is however unlikely that local radio will itself ever be involved in campaigning on particular issues: the statutory impartiality of the BBC and the commercial priorities of the IBA stations would seem to preclude this. In the last analysis however, the degree of local radio's involvement in local affairs must depend very much on the extent to which the listening public identify it as a source of news and views. In terms of its functions in relation to local politics the key issue may be whether it can find itself a role alongside the very different roles performed by the established and the alternative press in their coverage of the subject.

As for television, the regional scale at which it operates currently precludes any coherent or sustained coverage of purely local issues. Some series such as Granada's 'On Site' and 'The London Programme' on London Weekend have attempted to discuss public issues at both the local and regional level. On the whole, coverage of specific local issues tends to resemble that of the press, with crises and confrontations suddenly emerging to be filmed, broadcast and forgotten. The occasional documentary programmes on the workings of a local council or one of its departments, whilst often making informative viewing, suffer from a similar lack of any permanent context of news and analysis within the medium. It might be that in an ideal world issues of local politics could be treated briefly and visually on television, in more detail and with greater personalisation on local radio, and critically and in depth in the local press (Robertson, 1974, p.34). We are however a very long way from attaining any such state of affairs. It is hard to avoid the conclusion that at the local level the performance of the media as a link between governors and the governed is barely adequate. This may however merely reflect the fact that both the media men and their audience make rather different demands on the media from those which public-spirited civic leaders would like them to make.

Local Elections

Notwithstanding the importance of the existence and operations of political parties, pressure groups and the media, it is the mechanism of free elections which is the foundation of any claim to a local government based upon representative democracy. Moreover, the notion of local government based upon elections is one which commands very wide support amongst the electors (CMLG, 1967, vol.3, table 97). Despite this however, turnout at local elections is notoriously low. For example in contested local elections in the 1950s and 1960s in England and Wales, turnout ranged from a low of 37.6 per cent to a high of 48.0 per cent, with the 1960s having on balance a lower turnout than the 1950s (Registrar General's *Statistical Review of England and Wales, 1951,* part II, table V; *1960,* part III, table CXXV; and *1970,* part II, table V2). These figures do not represent a specifically modern trend: complaints were voiced about local electoral apathy in the 1920s, 1930s and 1940s (Hasluck, 1948, pp.40-1). Other European countries boast better performances, with West Germany and Sweden for example averaging turnouts of 70 per cent and 80 per cent respectively (CMLG,

1967, vol.4, pp.29 and 146). The matter is not necessarily a question of apathy purely at local elections. Of the nine member nations of the European Economic Community, Britain (together with Ireland) ranks lowest in national election turnout (Rose, 1974b, p.97-8). Thus there is presumably some wider cultural influence at work over and above simple lack of interest in local elections. Nevertheless it is certainly true that most people believe that voting at general elections is more important than voting at local elections because of the major role of central government as compared with local government (RCC, 1973, Research Paper 7, table 12).

For the party workers who bear the brunt of the campaign activity local elections have been aptly described as 'a jamboree. . .one of a long series of annual acts of renewal' (Jones, in Sharpe, 1967, p.260) in which it is as true as it is of general elections that 'the expressive[4] elements of campaigning seem to be at least as significant as the instrumental one' (Kavanagh, 1970, p.96). In purely electoral terms there are of course instrumental goals to be pursued. In marginal wards the party's sitting councillors must be defended and opposition incumbents defeated: in safe or in hopeless wards the campaign must be waged to tie down the enemy's forces and to keep the electors in the habit of voting in the period between general elections. The morale of the party's workers must be maintained, and their efficiency sustained, in case of a sudden dissolution of Parliament and a call to national battle. 'Municipal elections in politics are the equivalent of Autumn manoeuvres in military affairs.' (Conservative MP quoted in Jones, 1969, p.47.)

The campaign itself is likely to fall into well-worn routines of canvassing, largely in those areas reckoned most favourable, addressing envelopes, delivering leaflets, manning polling stations and knocking up reluctant voters on the day of the election. At this level, large-scale poster campaigns, cavalcades, and public meetings are rare. Only GLC elections can support such activities, with Cabinet Ministers appearing on platforms to extol the virtues of their municipal colleagues, and hoardings proclaiming the rival merits of the parties.

Local elections lend themselves to a number of perpetual debates as to the best techniques of campaigning. Should election addresses emphasise the candidate or the policy of the party? Should they be produced individually for each ward, or centrally for the whole town, or at least in some recognisable house style? Should the candidates engage in letters to the correspondence column of the local paper? Should he rely on canvassing or should he make himself available at

home or on the phone to troubled ratepayers? Should each candidate
have a separate agent or will this cause the campaign to fall apart? To
party workers these issues can loom large at local elections because they
are not overshadowed, as at a general election, by the gladiatoral contest
being waged by Westminster politicians. There is thus a greater sense of
the conduct of the campaign being in the hands of purely local
politicians.

Coverage of local elections by the media is at best low key and
intermittent. Where there is only a weekly paper it may publish only
two or three times during any one campaign. There is thus neither the
number nor the frequency of issues to sustain a lively coverage of the
campaign. Even where there are daily papers coverage is often restricted
largely to statements by candidates and parties, biographical notes, and
editorial homilies on the voter's duties (Sharpe, 1967, *passim*). As such
it adds little to the information provided in the election addresses
issued to the householders by the candidates. Once again the GLC
provides the exception to this type of treatment, with the *Evening
Standard* coverage of the 1973 elections including a number of features
on individual constituency campaigns, a double page spread on party
prospects, a large number of news stories related to the elections, three
editorials, and – the final accolade – the temporary transfer of the
Political Editor from the Palace of Westminster to County Hall to
cover events.

For radio, reporting local elections is certainly a problem. The 'equal
treatment' requirements of the Representation of the People Act applies to
local as well as to general elections. How, in reality, could this be
applied to London's local radio stations when 5,000 candidates contest
1,800 seats in the London Borough elections? In 1976 the answer
devised by BBC Radio London was to select certain key themes of the
election and to have phone-in programmes directed to party spokesmen
with the occasional non-party candidate appearing. This satisfied the
parties, and generated a good supply of callers, but did so only at the
risk of glossing over local issues. Similar problems arise in other stations
serving large conurbations.

In 1973 the combined attentions of the party workers, the press
and local radio ensured that no fewer than 88 per cent of the London
electorate knew that there was a GLC election on, in the week before
polling day. But only 44 per cent knew when polling day was, and in
the event only 35.2 per cent actually cast their vote (National Opinion
Polls, 1973). This suggests that publicity alone is not the answer to
electoral apathy at local level.

The activities and publicity generated by the campaign may not merely fail however to produce a high poll: they may also fail to have any significant impact on the overall result of the election. Such is the conclusion to which one is led by the apparent tendency of local election results to show a nationwide trend, suggesting that in casting their vote the electors have responded less to local issues than to some nationally applicable criterion of party choice. This phenomenom is not peculiar to Britain alone (Walsh, 1969, p.22), nor is it in Britain, a very new discovery. In the late 1830s and early 1840s, the Conservative national agent, F.R. Bonham, 'kept a careful scrutiny of the municipal elections as pointers to the growing national strength of the party' (Gash, 1953, p.415), whilst a generation later John Gorst tried, without success, to impress Disraeli with the importance of local elections as a barometer of national public opinion (Hanham, 1959, p.389). During the nineteenth century, Hanham argues, municipal election results 'always reflected to some degree the shift in national political opinion, although the degree to which particular boroughs were affected depended on local circumstances' (ibid., p.388).

In modern times, there is considerable evidence that local election results — in areas of inter-party contested seats — continue to reflect the general standing of the national parties at the time (Sharpe, 1967, p.320; Gregory, 1969, p.42; Johnson, 1972, p.16; National Opinion Polls, 1973). Butler and Stokes observed from their survey of voters in 1963 that 'those who went to the polls in local elections that were fought on a party basis voted to an overwhelming degree in line with their expressed (national) party self-image. . .well over 90 per cent of our respondents stayed with their generalised ties to the national parties.' Moreover, four out of every five claimed that there were no specific issues which concerned them in the 1963 local elections, whilst the remainder mentioned matters which were more the concern of Westminster than of the local council. It was also observed that the more strongly partisan the voter the more likely he was to vote in the local elections (Butler and Stokes, 1975, pp.40-4).

In interpreting this state of affairs it will help to note Rose's comment that 'voting is not so much a spontaneous expression of political views by an individual wishing to initiate or advance interests, but rather an individual response, more or less passive, to continuing social influences' (Rose, 1974, p.104). Amongst these social influences that of social class remains the single most significant, even though it may be declining and sometimes muffled in its impact (Rose, 1974, ch.2; Rose, 1974c, ch.10; Pulzer, 1967, ch.4). As such class is an influence which transcends the boundaries and preoccupations of individual local authorities and leads to the situation described in Chester in 1964 where voting behaviour in the town wards revealed that 'party allegiance depended upon class and occupational divisions which reached back more than fifty years and were reflected in the physical layout of the town' (Lee, in Sharpe, 1967, p.86).

As a determinant of party loyalty social class is an influence which is not seriously weakened by local conditions. It thus provides the bedrock of local party support, and in simple terms explains why, for example, the Royal Borough of Kensington and Chelsea is very unlikely ever to have a Labour council. Upon this substructure of class-based party support there rests of course the superstructure which actually determines the relative national state of the parties, a superstructure composed of a shifting constellation of images of party performance in relation to the issues concerning the elector. This performance − or their own interpretations of it − may be seen as a further 'continuing social influence' which together with social class, outweighs specific local issues of which the media and the campaign have made the voter only dimly aware. At the 1973 GLC elections for example, it was the view of many politicians, journalists and environmentalists that the main issue of this particular campaign was the Motorway Box: yet electors were in fact more concerned about the traditional and nationwide problems of housing, rents, law and order, and the rates (National Opinion Polls, 1973). All these issues could be related to certain general images of the main parties and their performance in office, actual or likely, and it required no particular interest in local affairs to do so. Purely local issues, as perceived by the politicians and the media, and the local structures for handling those issues, do not impinge very clearly on the minds of the electorate, for most of whom politics in any form is at best a marginal concern. Although ostensibly selecting representatives to tackle particular issues of the day, in practice the voters are content to use the occasion of an election to express their own socio-political self-image and to pronounce in general terms on a party's fitness to govern. In doing so they make little distinction between local and national elections other than to recognise the greater consequence of the latter.

Although local elections are thus the occasion for a generalised, nationwide response by the electorate there are, as indeed at general elections, local variations from the norm. Green argues for example that swings in local elections can be broken down into three components, a national, a city-wide and a ward element, and that although the

national element may be much the largest, there is nevertheless room
for local variations arising from city-wide and ward factors.
Consequently he suggests that local issues may on occasion have a
marked effect on local election results (Green, 1972). In fact of course,
the ward and city components of the swing may reflect the efficiency
of party organisation at those levels rather than the impact of local
issues. It is certainly likely that aggregated figures of party gains and
losses of council seats nationwide, whilst reflecting the prevalent state
of public opinion at large, obscure many local deviations. For one thing
there seems to be a greater turnover of seats at local elections than at
general elections, partly because of voters switching from abstaining to
voting (or the reverse) and also due to the impact of minor and
non-party candidates. Fletcher suggests that locally seats held by
majorities of up to 20 per cent may change hands, compared with the
conventional notion of 5 per cent as the defining majority in a marginal
parliamentary seat (Fletcher, in Sharpe, 1967, pp.196-7). Given the large
pool of normally abstaining voters at local elections it seems plausible
that a dramatic local issue and/or effective party organisation could
affect the result of the election. Experience in a variety of towns —
Harrow, Ashford, Wolverhampton, West Hartlepool, Newcastle,
Lancaster and Dundee — does suggest that effective party organisation
notably by increasing turnout of party supporters through knocking-up,
can significantly reduce or overturn majorities, which on previous low
polls may have been quite small in absolute terms (Brown, 1968; Brown
et al., 1972, p.147; Jones and Rees, in Sharpe, L.J., 1967; Pimlott,
1972, and 1973; Bochel and Denver, 1971 and 1972: for a dissenting
view see Newton, 1972b, with a rebuttal by Denver and Hands, 1972
and a rejoinder by Newton). Similarly various local issues have been
identified as influencing the outcome of certain local elections — town
expansion in Ashford, a rent rebate scheme in Sheffield, town centre
shopping in West Hartlepool and possibly, though less certainly, rent
increases in Leeds and a dispute over a municipal swimming pool in
Reading (Brown *et al.,* 1972, p.147; Hampton, 1970, p.177; Rees in
Sharpe, 1967, pp.235-7; Green, 1972, p.54).

  The possible existence of such local issues and the potential for
organising victory through differential turnout may be the jokers in the
local electoral pack. Because of them it can be argued that councillors
'can never be certain that their future is assured: the national average
figures conceal numerous local election upsets' and therefore 'local
elections are a valid method of emphasising accountability and control'
(Redcliffe-Maud and Wood, 1974, p.20). This, however, presupposes

that local politicians see their situation as subject to local upset and that they see it in the same light as the electors who are called to judge them. It is by no means certain that this is the case. In any event the councillor's fear of possible defeat through differential turnout is not so much a device for securing accountability as a spur to better electoral campaign organisation. The notion of accountability through 'local election upsets' must rest on the assumption that such upsets are the outcome of local dissatisfaction over the councillor's performance – or that of his party – on some local issue or issues. If this were the case then accountability could be secured either by electoral defeat of offending councillors, or by the councillors mending their ways in time to avoid retribution at the polls.

The latter practice – 'anticipated reaction'[5] – assumes that councillors are aware of any likely hostile public reaction to their proposals. In some ways, though, councillors are well shielded from critical public opinion. Much of their opinion sounding is likely to take place amongst their political colleagues on the council and in the parties, whilst for wider contacts they are most likely to rely on canvassing in generally well-disposed localities or on informal discussions with sympathisers in clubs and pubs. Thus it can all too easily be the case, as in Glasgow, that 'the appraisal of constituents' opinions made by councillors are generally inaccurate' even when they are akin to the opinions of the councillors themselves (Budge *et al.,* 1972, p.104; cf. Gregory, 1969). In Kensington and Chelsea councillors generally encountered only the views of those who were likely to agree with them on local issues, and in any case they did not regard local party policy as important in determining the outcome of local elections (Dearlove, 1973, ch.9 and table 2). Similarly, amongst councillors involved in educational policy making in three London boroughs, there was hardly any discussion of the issues in terms of voter opinion or party electoral prospects; there was instead a consciousness of the importance of national rather than local issues in determining their fate at the polls (Kantor, 1974, pp.20 and 24). In any event if the senior councillors most involved in policy making are representing safe wards, local electoral fortunes may not loom very large in their considerations, especially if the local social structure ensures that the majority party is permanently entrenched through its reflection of traditional class voting habits.

It is of course possible in a politically marginal authority, with few safe seats, with councillors sensitive to opinion, with opinion clearly and forcefully articulated, and with a local issue so crucial as to threaten the traditional voting habits of a lifetime, that the politicians will accommodate themselves to local desires by the fear of electoral retribution. There can, however, be few authorities where all these criteria apply.

Where councillors are not moved by any form of anticipated reaction, their failure to obey the voters wishes should, if they are truly accountable, lead to their subsequent removal from office. Yet this presupposes that revenge over what may, by polling day, be already a *fait accompli,* will loom large enough in the voter's mind to outweigh such other considerations as his sense of class identity or his desire to pass an interim verdict on the national government of the day. There is no evidence that this situation is likely to occur. In fact the most dramatic examples of the voters rejecting wholesale their incumbent councillors have been the result not of local issues, but of national factors. The overturning of seemingly impregnable Labour majorities in the London borough elections of 1968 reflected a verdict of disillusionment with the Wilson government rather than with specific local Labour authorities (some of whom had provided adequate local material for disillusionment for a number of years without any noticeable electoral consequences).

It would be foolish to deny all possibility of local issues influencing electoral outcomes under specific circumstances such as those outlined above. In general, however, it seems to be the case that local election results are largely a reflection of national political trends, modified by the efficiency of party organisation and perhaps by fluctuations in the number of candidacies in ward contests. Accordingly the election of councillors does not operate as a satisfactory device for securing accountability for their actions on local problems. In fact local elections have become an enjoyable ritual for the party workers, an anointing for the councillors, and an act of civic piety for the more conscientious citizens.

Notes

1. RCC — Royal Commission on the Constitution.
2. 'Don't knows' totalled 21 per cent for counties, as against 4 per cent for districts and boroughs.
3. RCLGE — Royal Commission on Local Government in England.
4. i.e. fellowship, sense of purpose, excitement, involvement.
5. The term comes from Carl Friedrich (1937, p.203).

6 ACCOUNTABILITY AND PARTICIPATION

The political system of local government, as outlined in the preceding
chapters, can hardly be said to engage the active attention of the
majority of citizens. With only three-fifths of the electorate belonging
to local organisations, only two-fifths voting in local elections, only
one-fifth being even slightly active in local organisations, and with fewer
than 1 per cent ever having served, or stood for election, as a councillor,
local politics is clearly the preserve of a minority in the community.
Yet this minority operates a political system purportedly based on
notions of democracy which command wide support amongst the public
at large (CMLG, 1967, vol.III, tables 95, 96 and 97). In a sense, therefore,
the active minority are trustees of the idea of local democracy in which
the majority of their fellow citizens place their faith. This is particularly
true of that very small minority whose place within the political system
is secured by election – the councillors. For although pressure groups
and a free press may be important components of a democratic society,
it is the existence of freely elected representatives which is the singular
hall-mark of that form of democracy on which British local government
is based. If we are to make some assessment of the health of democratic
local government, it is the elected representatives who must be the
special focus of our attention. In examining how far councillors are able
to live up to the requirements of local democracy it will help us to
consider separately the two contrasting roles of 'tribune' and
'statesman' identified in Chapter 2.

The Councillor as Tribune: The Rise of the Surrogate

The councillor as tribune is primarily concerned with the casework and
the local problems that arise out of the ward he represents and out of
the various social groups and organisations with which he is actively
involved. He functions as the voters' watchdog over the bureaucracy
and as their errand-boy trying to deliver to them the municipal goods
and services they demand: he pleads the case for particular interests and
defends his own constituents against policies that may harm them.

In practice, this is not always an easy role to perform satisfactorily.
For one thing, the councillor from his earliest days, is soon socialised
into the realisation that his immediate constituents are not the only
claimants to his loyalty. The committees on which he serves, the party

group, the council as a whole, will all claim prior loyalty. Even though he may withstand these blandishments his more senior colleagues, actual or aspiring municipal statesmen, are all too likely to dismiss his own particular pleas as parochial axe-grinding. Even when he is concerned not to wrangle with his fellow councillors but to intercede with an officer he may find it harder than he knows. Certainly the close contact between members and officials, unparalleled at Westminster, makes it hard for the councillor to importune too vigorously and aggressively on a constituent's behalf without imperilling a close working relationship. (J.G. Davies cites the case of a chief officer who actually saw the councillor's role as defending officers against the public rather than the other way around (Davies, J.G., 1972b, p.114).) Since officers, unlike civil servants, may often be called upon to defend in public policies which are, at least in name, those of the politicians, it is hardly surprising that they should on occasion expect some reciprocal loyalty, even if this hampers the councillor in his role as watchdog. This is not to say that officers will invariably react adversely to any member taking up some local issue or constituent's complaint. Most officers are genuinely disposed to be helpful: others can see the political good sense of putting a member in one's debt occasionally. The problems arise when pursuit of a particular case by a member seems likely to call into question the efficiency or dedication or judgement or compassion of an officer. The persistent, nagging, sceptical councillor who won't rest until he and his constituents are satisfied is an irritant within a system which depends even more than central government on close interaction and co-operation between politician and bureaucrat.

Moreover, the formal structure of local government rather limits the ability of the councillor to operate as a lone trouble-shooter. Legally he has no rights to probe beyond those specific matters which the council have entrusted to him through his committee memberships: he has no grounds on which to demand access to the files whenever he chooses. Nor, of course, can he give an officer any directions as to how a case should be handled, since only the committees or the full council may instruct the officers. And in the last analysis the councillor is himself constitutionally responsible for all the decisions of his authority. Unlike the Member of Parliament who can criticise the executive from the independent standpoint of a legislator, the councillor is himself part and parcel of the executive even if he is merely a humble back-bencher.

It was recognition of the difficulties which exist in carrying out the watchdog function in local government which led to the creation of Local Commissioners for Administration — the Local Ombudsmen —

under the 1974 Local Government Act and 1975 Local Government
(Scotland) Act. The simultaneous re-organisation of local government
may also have encouraged such an innovation since, by increasing the
average number of electors per councillor, it made it somewhat harder
for the latter to do justice to his constituency. Although complaints to
the Commissioners must be forwarded through a councillor in the first
instance, the Commissions do provide an independent source of
investigation into local maladministration, a term covering 'neglect, bias,
unfairness, incompetence, excessive delay, or the use of faulty systems
for handling cases' (Department of the Environment, 1974, para.3). The
Commissions have, however, no powers of redress, their function being
to present to the local authority, and to the complainant, the councillor,
and any individual complained against, a report which must be made
public, and to which the authority must respond with proposals for
action. The basic sanction is that of publicity of the authority's
shortcomings.

The local authority associations were hostile to the appointment of
local ombudsmen since they saw it as usurping a traditional function of
the councillor. Conversely many MPs favoured an ombudsman system
which totally excluded the councillor, with complaints being directed
through themselves: they saw councillors as either unable to cope with
the task or as being possibly involved themselves in the subject under
investigation (Cohen, 1973). What does seem clear, is that rightly or
wrongly, the councillor has been found unable to deal adequately with
certain types of local grievance, and that accordingly a surrogate has
been provided in the form of the local ombudsmen.

This is not the first instance of the councillor's role of local case-
worker falling, in part, into other hands. Although they rarely get
involved in disputes over local authority policy, MPs do find themselves
in demand to sort out personal problems which their constituents face
in connection with the council. Whether MPs conduct surgeries or
merely rely on their post-bag to bring them their constituents'
problems, housing – a council responsibility – looms large amongst the
personal cases, with planning, education and welfare sometimes ranking
close to housing in volume (Cohen, 1973; Barker and Rush, 1970,
pp.173-89; Dowse, 1963; Dinnage, 1972; Hampton, 1970, p.80). This is
not a new phenomenom, since long-serving MPs recollect helping with
such matters in the 1930s and 1940s (Cohen, 1973). It may of course
reflect the greater public visibility of an MP compared with a councillor,
or confusion or ignorance as to the distinction between the two, or the
belief that the MP can bring greater weight to bear on the council than

a mere councillor, or even the fact that a councillor has already been approached and, for whatever reason, failed to satisfy. In any event it is clear that the local ombudsmen are following rather than creating a practice of supplementing the councillor with some form of surrogate case-worker.

The MP and the local ombudsmen are not indeed the sole instances of such councillor-surrogates. In recent years there have emerged a group of bodies designed to assist the citizenry in their dealings with the council. Housing Aid and Advice Centres, Planning Aid Centres, Neighbourhood Law Centres, Welfare Claimants Unions, together with bodies such as Shelter and the growing number of community action groups, exist to provide the public with the sort of information, advice and assistance which, in theory, their councillors ought to be able and willing to provide. The growth of such bodies suggests that the demand for this sort of service has expanded beyond the ability of the average councillor to handle it.

Not only are MPs, ombudsmen, Aid Centres and Community groups taking up part of the councillor's role as case-worker and watchdog: there are pressures for his role as local spokesman to be similarly shared. Parish Councils, the advocates of new Neighbourhood Councils, radical community groups, and the alternative press all urge their claims as the true voices of a local opinion which for some reason the councillor is thought not to articulate adequately. Even the established press makes its bid to represent the true state of public opinion better than the councillor (Jenkins, 1973a). The development of exercises in public participation with their opinion surveys, public meetings, community forums, consultation documents and the like similarly encroach on the councillor's role as local spokesman.

The task of the councillor as tribune is to represent his local ward as case-worker, as watchdog over the officials, and as the spokesman for local interests and opinions. The emergence of so many surrogates for the councillor in these respects suggests that he is increasingly unable to cope with the demands made on him in his role as tribune.

The Councillor As Statesman: Problems of Party Government

The hallmark of the councillor as statesman is his concern with the policy making activities of the local authority. This concern may vary in the degree of active participation in policy making which it entails. At one level the councillor might insist that policy making is the politician's prerogative, and might devote much time, along with his political colleagues, to devising policies in line with their shared political objectives. Or the councillor may be happy to leave policy initiation largely to the officers, concentrating his attention on examining the proposals they bring forward to ensure they are politically acceptable. Or yet again he may accept quite uncritically, whatever policies are put forward by the officers, deriving his satisfaction not from the content of the policy so much as from being 'in the know', 'pushing things through' and 'getting things done'. We may describe these three types of involvement in policy making as policy initiation, policy scrutiny, and policy acceptance. In a system of government which presupposes that the paid officials are subordinate to the elected representatives, one would assume that the councillor as statesman would be concerned with initiation of policy rather than with its mere scrutiny or acceptance. Such an active role implies that the councillor can formulate his goals and identify at least the broad strategies required to achieve them. Even if he is merely concerned with policy scrutiny rather than with policy initiation, this too presupposes that he can articulate his own goals sufficiently clearly for him to apply political criteria to the policies put forward by the officers.

The twin growth of a corporate approach to policy making and of party politics in local government suggests a key role for the party as a mechanism for enabling the statesman-councillor to function effectively in initiating or scrutinising policy and in securing its passage through the committees and the council. In practice, however, there are considerable obstacles to parties providing the sort of support or framework within which the statesman-councillor can work effectively as initiator or scrutineer of policy. In the context of Westminster, Rose has identified a number of obstacles to effective party government which can exist 'only in so far as the actions of office-holders are influenced by values and policies derived from the institutions of party', for otherwise 'the party reigns but does not rule' (Rose, 1974b, p.379). Although concerned with Westminster, Rose suggests that many of his observations on party government are applicable to local politics (Rose, 1974b, p.16). The requirements he lists for effective party government (Rose, 1974b, ch.XV and XVI) in fact provide a useful device for assessing how far the institution of party can help the statesman-councillor to function effectively.

The first requirement is formulating policy intentions and workable means to achieve desired ends. At the local level parties almost invariably lack the assistance of research departments, independent research and propaganda bodies (such as the Fabians or the Bow Group), and sympathetic academics which underpin the making of party policy at national level. Many parties contesting local elections have no equivalent of a general election manifesto, other than perhaps a list of slogans about keeping down the rates or abolishing the eleven-plus. Rarely are these slogans translated into a programme for action.

The problems involved in party policy making at local level can be seen from a rare and untypical example which proved to be one of the most successful such exercises in recent times. For the county elections of 1973 the Labour Party in Nottinghamshire produced a policy statement of some 75 pages totalling over 30,000 words. This represented work over a six-month period by six working parties involving some fifty party members (Minutes of the Nottinghamshire Temporary Co-ordinating Committee of the Labour Party, October 1971 to April 1973). Many of the same people were simultaneously involved in organising candidate selection procedures, planning electoral tactics, raising and spending money, preparing for and attending meetings of the party committees supervising the county campaign, serving on the existing local authorities, running their local party branches and of course earning their living and caring for their families. The working parties suffered from the occasional problems inevitable in policy making at this level. The environment and leisure working party found its council members were sometimes too busy to attend, the convenor of the information and consumer protection working party fell ill and had to be replaced, and the working party on planning and transportation had difficulty in obtaining the advice of a qualified planner. The fact that a comprehensive policy document was eventually produced, despite the pressures on those involved and the lack of expertise and resources, says much for the enthusiasm of those involved when faced with the challenge of setting up a new local authority. The experience was, however, almost certainly unique in both its scale and its outcome, representing a conjunction of the right men and the right hour. At other times and in other places the lack of expert advice and the competition from other demands on the time of amateur politicians tend to preclude all but the most perfunctory of attempts at formulating policies and the steps required to implement them.

If policies are to be implemented then the party must be capable of placing party nominees in the most important positions of government, and in large enough numbers to have an effect. In practice, this means, in the context of local government, ensuring that party nominees secure the committee chairmanships and that the party controls the committees as well as the council. The latter is largely a mere exercise in applied political arithmetic and should cause little difficulty. More problematical is the matter of the chairmanships. It is not enough to have these posts under party control; those who occupy them must do so actively. They must be able to monitor what is going on in the relevant departments, give political guidance on sensitive issues, and ensure that party policies are being implemented. In a large authority this role requires in effect a full-time chairman. The days are vanishing when the chairman can rely on occasional phone-calls to, and lunch with, the chief officer and still hope to be more than a figure-head.

As for how many partisan nominees are required for effective party government this involves more than questions of committee chairmanships. It raises the question of how far such chairmen, or party leaders, need additional hands, ears and eyes in order to keep the local authority machine moving on the approved course. The appointment of personal and research assistants at the GLC and in Nottinghamshire, although not done on a partisan basis, gives the statesman-councillor the beginnings of a private office. The appointment of purely political assistants, as for the leader of the GLC, is a more overtly partisan move which may create some difficulties in terms of relations with the officials (Walker Interview). These innovations have yet to be fully tested. What does seem clear, however, is that until recently party politicians have rarely thought at all about how far they, as committee chairmen, could really keep on terms with the chief officers and their departments. There has been very little discussion on the functions and requirements of chairmen as party politicians. This may of course merely reflect the lack of specific party policy remitted to their charge.

One requirement of the successful local politician is that of possessing the skills necessary to control large bureaucratic organisations. Traditionally the skills of the successful politician have been those of discussion and debate, negotiation and compromise: they are diplomatic rather than managerial skills. Few councillors have much experience of running large organisations, and those that do may have gained their experience in the rather different world of private enterprise. The legal and professional language and preoccupations of the officers are often alien to the local politician, who, moreover, rarely has the time or the facilities to overcome his lack of understanding. The growing use of management techniques in local government poses a particular problem in that it adds a third language to the legal and professional languages which have traditionally dominated local authorities. The past experience, in his party or in voluntary organisations, which a councillor brings to his council work may have equipped him well to deal with his fellow politicians, with the media and with party workers and pressure groups.

On the whole these groups talk a similar language of the clash of interest and of conflict and compromise. Council officers are more used to discussing efficiency or propriety than problems of equity or distributive justice. Given that councillors mostly lack managerial skills, and that they neither share a common policy language[1] with their officers nor have a generalist mediator to bridge the gap it can be difficult for them to bend the bureaucracy to their will. If they are to do so they must be able to produce crystal clear political instructions which admit little ambiguity in interpretation and whose implementation can be properly monitored. As already indicated this requirement makes too heavy a demand on most local politicians and their parties.

One factor in a party's ability to influence policy making is how far it can give a high priority to carrying out party policies. During the elected four-year lifetime of any one council, it is likely to find itself initially committed to a whole series of capital and revenue expenditures originally planned by its predecessors but now too far into the pipeline of design stage, tenders, contracts and appointments to be halted. As time goes by the constraints of this nature may lessen, to be replaced by the differing constraints of problems and circumstances never foreseen when election manifestos (if any) were being prepared two or three years previously. The emphasis on planning in the social services, in education, in transportation and in the environment renders more difficult any sudden changes in aims and objectives which entail lengthy reappraisals and re-writing of hitherto approved plans. Thus the combined impact of inheritance, inertia and the unforeseen can become alibis for failing to change policies in the supposedly desired direction. Only a firm commitment to specific policy changes can overcome these hurdles.

The final requirement for effective party rule is that party policies must be put into practice by the personnel of the regime. Officers are not normally on the lookout for trouble. They will be happy to continue traditional policies or to invent their own with the acquiescence of the members. They will advise, warn and discourage if politicians seem about to launch into initiatives that bristle with difficulties. But if the councillors persist with adamantine clarity in their proposals the officers will, with greater or lesser degrees of enthusiasm, put them into practice.

If there is one refrain which runs through the previous paragraphs it is that party government can be effective locally only if the party and its councillors know their own mind and have the political will to impose their ideas on the council machinery. But this in turn requires that both parties and party groups establish clear aims and objectives and means of achieving them. It is simply but sadly rare for local politicians and their parties to command the levels of information, expertise, manpower and time to prepare comprehensive policies. In practice they must rely on the officers reacting intelligently to the often simplistic slogans on which the local politicians have campaigned. Sometimes this will produce a course of action which the party would have advocated had it had the resources to identify it. All too often however the parties are left 'justifying whatever is formally done in their name' by the officers (Rose, 1974b, p.1).

For the councillor as statesman, party offers itself as a countervailing force to the ideas and influence of the officers. Yet it is too often a vague and fitful guide to action, providing him with half-formed glimmerings of what a policy might be. As a result the statesman-councillor is rarely the initiator of policies. He is either the scrutineer of the officers' proposals, examining them in the light of the traditions and experience of the party and the social groups to which he belongs, or at worst he is the mere acceptor and guarantor of such proposals, dazzled by the officers' expertise, and expediting their schemes with such self-abnegating disclaimers as 'we have to trust our officers, that's what we pay them for'.

The Problem of Accountability

Under the contemporary system of representative democracy the prime vehicles of accountability to the public are the elected member and the political party, representing the individual and the collective agents upon whose performance the voters can pronounce at the polls. As we have seen, in the context of local government, the performance of these two agents is somewhat imperfect.

The inability of the councillor to perform adequately his duties as a case-worker, as a watchdog and as a local spokesman, has led to the emergence of a variety of surrogates to supplement or to replace him. The ability of the councillor to determine policy effectively is hampered by his lack of the necessary time, information and resources, and by the failure of the political parties to provide him with any substantial alternative to reliance upon his officers.

Political parties themselves may of course perform a variety of functions in any given political system (cf. Jupp, 1968). In the case of local politics they do perform valuable services in terms of recruitment to the council, the representation of certain social groups and the aggregation of their interests, and the organisation of the internal workings of the local authority. They are, however, all too prone to fail when they are faced with moving beyond sloganising into the formulation of policy.

Given the imperfection of their performance it might be expected that councillors and parties would be constantly meeting retribution at the polls. Yet the reality is very different. The results of local elections are generally a reflection of national rather than local situations. Their outcome is largely in the hands of Westminster, and is thus beyond the control of the local politicians. As a result, for the councillor, electoral defeat is not so much a vehicle of accountability as a visitation akin to death – a phenomenom whose possible occurrence must be acknowledged but whose incidence cannot be planned against, and which is therefore rarely a factor in decision taking. There may be occasional local election upsets but these may well be due to efficient campaign organisation or to changing candidacy patterns, not simply to local issues. Even if councillors were tempted to play safe against local upsets by anticipating the possible reaction of their constituents to local issues, it is by no means certain that they can estimate correctly the nature of the reaction. Thus local elections rarely prove to be effective devices for securing accountability, not least of course because the voters prefer to use them for the purpose of expressing their feelings on matters which are not local.

In between elections, moreover, councillors can be remarkably well insulated from public sentiment, communicating primarily with each other and with their officers rather than with the public, relying on the party organisations and on the more well-disposed and thus more favoured pressure groups for expressions of opinion, and generally socialising and canvassing amongst those most likely to, at very least, give them the benefit of the doubt. The parties and the pressure groups, moreover, represent at best an active minority of the electorate and have little day-to-day control over the councillor's actions. As for the media they do not normally adopt an analytic or investigatory stance towards local politicians, whom they may occasionally irritate but rarely influence.

In practice then local politicians are remarkably autonomous and unaccountable performers, for all the imperfections of their performance. Even were they in some ways more accountable, there would still remain some problems concerning the nature of that accountability.

The emphasis in notions of accountability lies in providing a 'post-mortem of action' (Normanton, 1971, p.312) offering 'the possibility of expressing censure and of fixing blame' (Johnson, 1974, p.6). There is also the corollary that once blame has been affixed, the offenders can be removed from office and policies changed. This may well be plausible in national politics, where industries can be nationalised and de-nationalised, legislation repealed, and foreign and defence policies amended if not altered: even here, though, the room for manoeuvre may not always be large. For local government a major problem is that many of the most controversial policies cannot easily be undone once put into operation. Roads cannot be unbuilt; reorganised schools cannot be readily unscrambled; demolished houses cannot be reconstructed; industrial estates cannot be turned back to green fields; tower blocks cannot be converted into two-storey terraces; homes for the mentally handicapped and schools for the maladjusted cannot be moved around from one site to another; overspill families cannot be shipped back to the metropolis whence they came. Thus even if local residents were able effectively to apportion blame for decisions they disliked and then to dismiss from office those politically responsible, they might still be unable to secure the reversal of the decisions themselves. Not only are local politicians largely unaccountable, even if they were accountable their works may endure long after their dismissal from office. This may help to explain the growing demand over the past decade, not merely for true accountability after the event, but for prior authorisation by the community through public participation.

Public Participation

Historically the election of representatives has been the primary device for enabling the public to participate in decision making in government, supplemented from time to time 'by petition, by agitation or by riot' (Perkin, 1973, p.6). During the 1960s Britain shared with other Western industrialised societies the emergence of demands for more effective mechanisms of participation than those traditionally employed. A number of reasons could be advanced for this development, although they are all open to the charge of relying on the illogic of *post hoc ergo propter hoc.*

The growth of secondary and further education, the development of the mass media, the emergence of certain issues, for example those of morality or the environment, which seemed to cut across traditional party loyalties, and the trend towards larger units, greater rationality, greater integration and more comprehensive planning by government agencies, may all have combined to give the public a greater awareness of what was being done in their name and a greater sense of remoteness from those who were doing it. More generally, there may have developed a realisation that the power and resources of public bodies had made them into major agents of accelerating social change and that these bodies although supposedly under democratic control were not always producing the social changes desired by the public. The fact that the demands for more participation were especially strident in the field of local planning may thus reflect the fact that planning produced the most readily visible — and once completed often the least reversible — forms of social change, removing, or rehousing, familiar faces and destroying familiar places.

Demands for more participation do not in themselves define what procedures or structures are desirable. Thus various schemes may be devised which purport to effect public participation but which lie at varying points along a continuum from cynical manipulation of the public at one end, through consultation and partnership, to total citizen control (Arnstein, 1971). Similarly, the established authorities may see the purpose of participation rather differently from its more radical advocates. The merits of participation in planning were justified by the Skeffington Committee by its contribution to shortening the time-scale of planning through reducing the number of objections (Ministry of Housing and Local Government, 1969, paras.174-5, 191, 238). Other forms of participation, such as tenant management of housing, or self-management of day centres for the elderly, may be welcomed more as a means of saving the council money and staff than as an exercise in pure democracy: the corollary of course is that if such experiments lead to demands for more resources because of the discovery of hitherto unexpressed needs, relations may become rather strained.

As currently practised it is possible to distinguish two main types of participation which occur under the aegis of local authorities. One, which might be termed administrative participation, involves the members or patrons of a particular institution, for example a housing estate, a school or a day centre, in its administration (cf.Ward, 1974). The other is concerned not with administration but with consultation, seeking the views of the public about plans and proposals for particular localities.

It may be the case that success is rather easier to achieve in administrative than in consultative participation. Any sustained involvement in participation requires the sacrifice of time and effort which might be employed in other ways. Studies in the USA have suggested that participation may depend on the stakes which individuals feel they have invested in a particular situation (Davies, J.C., 1966, pp.154-67; Kaplan, 1963, pp.136-9; Rossi and Dentler, 1961, ch.8). Residents on an estate or parents with children in a school may find it comparatively easy to identify the stake they have in the management of the estate or the school. To identify their various stakes in any of a number of strategic options presented as part of a consultation on an urban structure plan may be much more difficult (cf. Perkins and Barnes, 1975). Certainly the evidence suggests that public involvement in consultative participation is still at a fairly low level. A survey by National Opinion Polls discovered that amongst those who were aware of any participation exercise conducted by their local council only 12 per cent had in fact participated by returning questionnaires, or visiting an exhibition or attending a public meeting. Moreover this active minority of participators were more middle class, more well-educated, more likely to be members of political parties or pressure groups, and more likely to have had previous experience of complaining to the council than the average citizen: in other words, they were largely the same minority as used to participate before the days of 'participation' (National Opinion Polls, 1975).

This latter finding raises the important question of whether the social balance of participation is more important than the overall level of participation. If the aim of participation is to ensure that a wide cross-section of views is expressed from all quarters, then market research techniques may well be more effective than current exercises in participation which rely on the public coming forward to the council rather than the council seeking out the public. Such an approach might result in fewer (because of the cost) but more representative individual views being expressed by the public. However, it would clearly fail to satisfy those for whom participation is not solely an instrumental device for securing the expression of views but is also an expressive and developmental device for securing a greater sense of political identity, awareness and self-confidence amongst both individuals and communities.

Community Action

A combination of the instrumental, expressive and developmental approaches to public participation is found in community action, which also often embraces measures of both administrative and consultative participation. The focus of community action is the limited but all-inclusive territorial community, rather than the fragmented or partial constituencies of council tenants or old-age pensioners or those who happen to be directly affected by particular planning proposals.

An emphasis on the local community is one which has been present in much central government legislation and policy of the past decade. Educational priority areas, action areas for planning, general improvement areas for housing, area teams for the social services, community development projects sponsored by the Home Office, all these have emerged almost as if to counter the simultaneous trend to larger, more rational, and more remote units of administration. Generally however, their aim was to provide more effective public services rather than to encourage local democracy. At local government level there have emerged a variety of community development activities, linked for example with social work, with adult education, and with urban renewal or new town housing projects. The significance of the small-scale community is not lost on the public at large either, for research has shown that nearly four electors in five claim some sense of attachment to a 'home' community area, which in urban areas is usually no larger than a single ward and often no more than a group of neighbouring streets (RCLGE, 1969, Research Study 9; RCLGS, 1969, Research Study 2, Section A).

The particular characteristic of community action has been its emphasis on what people can do for themselves rather than on what the official authorities can do for them, and also its rejection of the traditional processes of party politics as an avenue of influence and action. In some ways, its emergence resembles that at national level of bodies such as Shelter, the Child Poverty Action Group, Age Concern and the like.

In its underlying philosophy and in its tactics community action exhibits some internal divergences. One model of community action adopts a consensual approach, with an emphasis on bargaining and negotiating with authority whilst the other is based on conflict and on tactics of confrontation such as demonstrations, sit-ins, squatting and other forms of direct action (Smith and Anderson, 1972; Bryant, 1972). There are similar though not necessarily parallel, divisions in the extent of radical ambition attaching to community action. Thus Rein sees community action 'as a strategy for building constituencies and thus altering the level and the distribution of resources' (Rein, in Lapping, 1970, p.14), a notion that has a fairly traditional political ring to it even if its emphasis is implicitly egalitarian: in contrast, Binns talks of the possibility that community action, 'by raising the right demands in the right ways,. . .can bring about a questioning of the priorities of this society and hence the possibility of its overthrow' (Binns, 1973, p.13).

The radicalism of many of the more articulate activists and theoreticians of community action should not however be allowed to obscure the fact that on occasion its preoccupations can be almost conservative in its defensive concern for protecting communities against unwanted change. So too, much of its hostility to planners and bureaucrats merely echoes more forcefully and perhaps with rather more insight, the traditional conservative antagonism towards the power of the state. Nor should any emphasis on a united community be allowed to obscure the fact that internal divisions can arise because of the differing perceptions and interests of, for example, tenants and owner-occupiers or indigenous and immigrant residents in a locality (see for example Coates and Silburn, 1970).

Nevertheless, despite the divisions and the confusions that may exist within it, community action both in style and content, does represent, even more than other forms of participation, a direct challenge to the normal system of local elected representation, and to the inability of the political parties to make that system work, especially in areas of urban deprivation. In the last analysis however, the posture of challenge cannot be maintained indefinitely without frustration and weariness setting in. It may be kept up longest by those who combine a dogged belief in ultimate revolution with a faith in the catalytic ability of community action to radicalise the workers. For those with less revolutionary aims the central problem is that although local community groups may sometimes be able to veto distasteful proposals for their locality, there is a limit to the net gains, in terms of resource distribution, which can be achieved through this form of micro-politics, especially if rich localities also organise in their own interests. Donnison (1973, p.394) observes that:

...those who would on principle reject collaboration with government and administration and professional innovation in favour of purely political strategies of action are putting their faith in (political) free enterprise in a (political) market-place. And in Britain those who do best in the economic market place will generally come out on top in a political free-for-all too.

We are thus led back to the need for micro-political action to relate to the larger scale macro-politics of the local authority where decisions about the differential distribution of resources between individual communities can be taken. But in doing so we are also led back to the problem of the difficult relationship between new concepts and foci of popular participation and the institution of traditional representative democracy.

Participation and the Council's Decisions

Many of the problems involved in trying to harmonise the claims of

public participation with those of existing institutions of local
government arise no doubt because the local authorities themselves are
not geared to cope with the new situation. In the normal course of
evolving plans and proposals within the local authority all manner of
negotiations, commitments and clearances have to be gone through. The
view from within the local authority is well summed up by Jay (1972, p.9):

> . . .look at the plan from the standpoint of the men who drew it up.
> They have been at it for months. It has generated several major
> internal rows. There have been long-negotiated compromises with
> other departments. The chap who started it all off was promoted
> half-way through and moved to Edinburgh. The first draft was
> produced in a tremendous rush because the Chairman of the Planning
> Committee didn't give the go-ahead till three months after the
> deadline date, and some of the flaws didn't show up until it was too
> late to do anything. The policy decision it stems from was taken six
> years ago, and they are now talking about rethinking the whole
> policy on a more comprehensive basis, so if it does not go through
> quickly it may never make it. It has meant a great deal of work and
> unpleasantness and getting home late for supper, and the thought of
> going back to square one gives them all nightmares.
>
> And yet, for all that, they are proud of it; proud at least of
> themselves for having turned out such a plausible and workmanlike
> job in the face of all the difficulties. Of course it has flaws, but they
> are well disguised. Of course it will be attacked, but all plans are
> attacked. And on the whole, they have come to believe that as a
> practical project in an imperfect world it is probably the best one
> around.

Clearly the process of attempting to tack a venture in participation on to
the end of such an exercise in plan preparation is likely to generate a
strong resistance to any changes in the plan should these be proposed by
the public. The council is, psychologically at least, committed to its
own proposals (cf. Levin, 1973).

Ideally of course such an impasse can be avoided by involving the
public at an earlier stage, whilst options are still numerous and before
any preferred strategies have begun to emerge which might generate
official commitment. However, this does not solve all the problems.
Certainly, presenting the public with a genuine choice between alternative
proposals is more in keeping with genuine participation than presenting
them with one proposal only. Nevertheless, there then emerges the

problem of how many options to be presented. Who is to say what the range of options is, or which ones are relevant or realistic?

Whether the public is being told 'this is the best solution' or 'these are the variety of possible solutions' there still arises the question of who is to say which solution or solutions are to be contemplated. Much of the discussion on participation is rightly concerned with the process of decision making and with identifying the stages at which the public can be involved. But concentration on the 'making' of decisions in the sense of the inputs or ingredients in the decision making process, may ignore the need for the 'taking' of decisions. At some point, or points, during the process, discussion must stop, propositions must be agreed, and the next course of action be identified. Politics concerns action as well as discussion. At a given point somebody has to call deliberations to a halt and to take the decision that X shall be done rather than Y or Z. Moreover, unless such a decision once taken is to be open to perpetual threat of revocation whoever takes the decision must be accepted as being the legitimate and authoritative decision taker. In a word, he must possess identifiable and acceptable credentials as the taker of decisions.

Such credentials may of course take a variety of forms in different societies — age, wealth, social position, physical strength, special knowledge might all be such credentials in different places at different times. In local government the credential has been that of securing election. It is by virtue of election that the councillor has claimed the right to take authoritative decisions. The more ambitious the claims for public participation, the more this credential is devalued. It is, however, devalued without being adequately replaced. To say that the 'people' rather than the councillor shall decide provides us with no operationally useful credential with which to identify the people, despite the manifold claims of demonstrations, public meetings, pressure groups and community activists to represent the real will of the people. Unless and until such credentials are discovered, the relationship between elected local politicians and the processes of public participation will remain one of permanent unease. In the last analysis the local politician, in conflict with particular manifestations of public opinion, will always be able to rest his case on the credential of his election. As we have seen it is in some ways an unsatisfactory credential since it provides him with authority without accountability. But so far we have found nothing with which to replace it, and the prospects for doing so seem poor.

Notes

1. The term is used by Solesbury (1974, pp.53-65) in connection with the manner in which policies are *expressed:* the term is used here to refer to the manner in which they are *conceived* and *discussed.*

7 THE FUTURE OF LOCAL POLITICS

The previous chapters have outlined the characteristics of various actors within the political system of local government, and have identified some of the problems arising from their interaction. It would be attractive to be able to prophesy how these problems will be resolved. This, however, seems to be an impossible task.

For one thing, the new authorities which recently came into existence are still in a sense on trial: until they have been in operation for a good number of years it will be hard to assess how well they function and how far they have affected the previous patterns and traditions of local politics. The devolution of power from Westminster is a subject which has been spoken of at almost wearisome length with little to show for it: yet if it should come to pass its consequences for the workings of local politics could be of great significance. The problem of local government finance may be resolved in ways which affect the powers and duties of local authorities. The very agenda of local politics may come under increasing pressure for change in the wake of both radical criticism of traditional policies for handling urban problems (Harvey, 1973; Pahl, 1970; Simmie, 1974), and of essentially conservative criticism of the scope of local authority services from leaders of the ratepayers' revolt.

Given the uncertainty which thus surrounds the immediate future of local politics prophecy is dangerous. Nevertheless, some thoughts on the future may reveal the possible outcomes if certain current trends were to continue. The developments outlined below are speculations. Although presented separately they are not always incompatible one with another and components of some of the developments could be combined with those of others. They have in common the property of reflecting present problems of representative democracy at the local level.

The Councillor as Figurehead

A situation could emerge in which the councillor was increasingly relegated to playing little more than a symbolic role in local politics. Given the growing scale and complexity of local government operations the part-time amateur politician, with few resources of his own, and with inadequate party backing or guidance, could easily become a mere dignified symbol. With his 'tribune' role taken over by a variety of

151

surrogates and his 'statesman' role surrendered to the officers, he is already perhaps some distance along that road. With a continuing growth of public participation in all its forms, there could develop a situation where there was indeed little for the councillor to do but formally to ratify agreements reached by the officers with groups of citizens outside the formal structure of the local authority.

Growing devolution of decision making powers in the area of administrative participation would reduce his involvement in many matters of detail, for example in questions concerning the running of housing estates. In terms of consultative participation, the way is open for an undermining of the councillor's right to speak for his electorate. An increasing use of market research techniques could give the council's officers a far clearer picture of public opinion than could casual soundings-out by a hard-pressed councillor. Already officers are not above claiming that they understand the public's views or needs better than do the elected representatives (cf. Kogan, 1973, p.88). Access to opinion research can make this claim a reality. Moreover, it is often the officers rather than the councillors who are called upon to present policies and proposals at public meetings and to address local societies, and thus to interpret technicalities and feasibilities to the laymen. Such direct contact between citizens and officers provides another instance of the councillor being bypassed as lay representative. The problem of assessing how far pressure groups really reflect sectional interest might be overcome by, for example, requiring them to register details of their aims and membership, in exchange for guaranteed access to specified stages in decision making or for the financial assistance advocated by the Stevenson Report (Department of the Environment, 1972a). With such a means of assessing the significance of pressure group views they would be more clearly established alongside opinion surveys as channels of communication. The councillor might then be left articulating little more than his own personal views.

Yet traditionally, a major role of the councillor has been to pronounce the nature of the public interest, as he sees it, over and against the partial and conflicting views of various sectional groups within the community. So long as these latter views were uttered in a low key, on infrequent occasions, and with due deference, it was all too easy for the councillor to ignore them. But the emergence of vocal and articulate minorities, and the prospect of plumbing, by survey, the opinions of the mass of electors could make it less and less credible for the councillor to claim that his definition of the public interest is universally or even widely accepted.

It would of course still be possible for councillors to carry on regardless, heedless of opinions other than their own. On current form they might well escape electoral retribution which we have seen to be a most uncertain weapon. Nevertheless, by losing the power to claim that they alone speak with the voice of the people, they lose their major moral advantage in their dealings with officers, and of course, with the general public. Moreover, the whole ethic of participation, be it administrative or consultative, is one of co-operation between the council and the community, rather than one of the council imposing its own will on the community. This becomes increasingly significant if the growing labour costs of local government services encourage councils to develop wide-ranging measures of administrative participation for economic as much as for democratic reasons. Once councils become dependent on tenants, parents and good neighbours, to help run their housing, educational and social services, in addition to the usual voluntary organisations, the emphasis on co-operation between the council and the public is strongly enhanced.

In such a situation the role of the councillor is reduced from that of providing leadership to at best that of a diplomat, a broker, and a go-between, seeking to bring conflicting groups together, to accommodate demands, and to ratify proposals acceptable to those directly affected. At worst even this role becomes superfluous if it can be carried out effectively by direct contact between the participating public and officers accustomed to gauging local opinion and negotiating with local interests.

Prevented from operating effectively as a 'tribune' or as a 'statesman', the councillor may find that in addition a developed system of public participation deprives him of his ultimate moral credentials as spokesman for the citizens, and thus renders it impossible for him to act effectively as an elected representative. He would thus have little real function left to perform. He might linger on for some time, to reign but not to rule, before his true irrelevance was admitted, or he might be abolished, which is of course the ultimate logic of participatory democracy in its purest form.

The Councillor in Control

It is not inevitable, however, that councillors will tamely acquiesce in the further whittling away of their position. There are, as we have seen, already signs that councillors on certain local authorities are instead trying to equip themselves with the resources necessary to ensure greater control by the elected members over policy making. Any serious attempt

by councillors to exert the full measure of political control to which
they are nominally entitled seems likely to involve a number of
developments. These include the emergence of some full-time, salaried
councillors; the development of adequate research and secretarial
resources for councillors; the provision of educational facilities to
enable councillors to keep abreast of developments in particular local
government services; the introduction of some variety of political/
personal/generalist assistance to leading councillors; the evolution of
committee chairmanships into posts of quasi-ministerial status at local
level; one-party policy committees; and a recognition by political
parties of the need to devote more resources to local politics.

The last of these developments may prove to be both the most
essential and the most difficult to bring to fruition. If councillors are
to sustain a commanding role *vis-à-vis* the officers and the various
participating publics, they will need to justify it on more adequate
grounds than those of constitutional propriety or concern for their own
personal position. Potentially the political parties could provide one such
justification. In a local authority where the councillor was a mere
figurehead — or even non-existent — decisions would be liable to reflect
little more than piecemeal compromises and accommodations between
various groups of professional officers and their clients amongst the
public. It would thus be hard to establish effective overall priorities
and to develop co-ordinated policies to deal with interconnected
problems. The risks of sectional myopia amongst officers and their
departmental publics would be very great. Political parties which were
able to develop local aims and strategies based on their own ideologies
and interests could in contrast provide coherent guidelines for corporate
policy making. They would thereby give their councillors a significant
role as expositors and expeditors of a local authority policy based on
some form of political analysis and preference.

However, such a role for the parties clearly makes great demands
on them in terms of resources. At present the ability of local party
organisations to handle policy formulation is of a fairly low order. They
would need to develop closer links with sympathisers in local polytechnics
and universities. The regional and area organisations of the parties would
need to concern themselves with more than organisational details, perhaps
acquiring their own research departments. Moreover, the party branches
might be well advised to bring themselves into closer and more frequent
touch with local opinion, whether by survey, or through liaison with
local societies, community groups and the like.

Certainly, if there is any meaning at all to notions of devolution of decision making in government away from Westminster, it should also entail a parallel redistribution of party resources and concern away from Smith Square to local branches. In the present parlous state of party finances this seems hard to envisage. It might however be borne in mind if any arrangements for state subsidies to the parties are seriously contemplated.

It is not only the political parties which will come under some pressure if councillors are to effectively dominate local government. The officers will also have adjustments to make. The traditional officers' complaint that on occasion 'members do not listen to our advice' will perhaps become more frequent, not because advice is not listened to but because councillors, with the bit between their teeth, will listen to it and then decide differently in the light of their own political priorities. Officers will have to get used to committee chairmen who see their role not merely as one of popping into the Town Hall for consultation if the chief officer has a tricky problem on hand, but who see themselves as prime movers and progress chasers on policy issues, with perhaps in the larger authorities their own office and personal staff.

In addition, officers may expect to deal with issues whose political consequences have to be laid bare rather than obscured in the 'neutral' language of professional expertise. Admittedly officers at present frequently claim to be very much alive to the political implications of their actions. However, they are often talking in terms of the internal politics of the authority — will this upset the chairman? Does this mean a clash between two committees? Is there going to be a split in one of the party groups over a particular proposal? In future, if councillors are really in control of policy, officers will need to talk of the consequences of different policies for the community outside the Town Hall in the political terms of gains and losses by different social groups. At present it is rare for them to do so. Thus for example, this writer's attempts to find out as a councillor who benefits, and who loses, from the maintenance of a Green Belt policy have been to no avail simply because the question has never before been posed in such terms and consequently no evidence has ever been gathered which might answer it. In future, if councillors take control with a clear commitment to specific policies officers will need to be prepared to answer questions of this nature.

If councillors are to take control in the way here suggested the consequences will not be felt solely by the officers and the political parties. One result may be the emergence of divisions amongst the councillors themselves. Reference has already been made (page 33 above) to the possibility that corporate planning may tend to separate out two different roles for the councillor, to formalise as it were the roles of statesman and tribune. The development of full-time committee chairmen with quasi-ministerial status and the use of one-party policy committees could well accentuate this trend, leaving the majority of councillors to deal with case-work whilst the minority concentrate on policy making.

However, it might be argued that case-work is all that councillors should realistically aspire to deal with, that policy-making involves so many technicalities that councillors can make no effective contribution and that their political parties will not in practice equip them so to do. If this should be the case, then a third possible development presents itself, namely the conversion of councils (as bodies of elected representatives) into watchdog bodies or consumer councils, with no pretensions to policy making and engaged solely in deliberation, investigation and scrutiny.

The Council as Consumers' Forum

The idea of making specific provision for a permanent watchdog body in local government was adopted by the Maud Committee, who intended this to be the prime task of council committees in relation to the proposed policy making management board. However the situation under these proposals would have been in effect one of internal dialogue between two sets of councillors. If the policy making role of the councillor is abandoned entirely, then the dialogue becomes one between the officers, who make and implement policies, and the watchdog councillors representing the consumers who experience the policies in action.

This latter notion of lay persons representing the consumer to public officials is not of course entirely new. It is to be found in the consumer councils of the nationalised industries and in the more recently created Community Health Councils within the National Health Service. The functioning of the consumer councils has come in for some considerable criticism (Consumer Council 1968; Select Committee on Nationalised Industries 1971). Their existence is largely unknown to the general public, their relationships to their various industries is too close (e.g. sharing staff and premises), their terms of reference are too narrow, their own resources for research and investigation are inadequate. Moreover the members of the councils are not, even in theory, in any way accountable other than to the Minister who appoints them. Even those members who are required by statute to come from local authorities (a proportion varying between 40 and 60 per cent) are under no obligation to develop specific links with the local community or to report back to it. In short, as a device for linking local consumers and public corporations, the present consumers' councils have no responsibility to any form of political constituency, which may in turn explain why they have evoked so little public interest in their activities or their inadequacies.

If these consumer councils require to be more firmly rooted in a local political constituency, then one solution could be to base them in some way directly on the local authorities (cf. Griffith, 1950). However, we have been contemplating the possibility of the traditional local councillor becoming exclusively concerned with his role as consumer's champion in respect of the normal local authority services. The possibility now arises of combining all the various local consumer representation roles into one single consumer forum, directly elected by the voters and representing them as users of all the services of the traditional local authority, the nationalised industries and the health service.

To perform at all adequately such a body would clearly need its own financial resources, and its own staff and research facilities. It would in effect need to develop its own 'counter-bureaucracy' to enable it to act as an effective counter-force to the established authorities. Given this, it would be able to make representations on behalf of local consumers, to monitor the performance of the authorities supplying local public services, to report general public reaction to different types and levels of service, and to evaluate and criticise the policy assumptions of the various authorities. Such a body might also take under its wing the present work of Consumer Protection in relation to private traders, along with the provision of advice and information at present carried out by Advice Bureaux and Aid Centres. It might also become the recognised mechanism of consultation by central government on issues of local significance such as proposals to close down factories or develop new industries.

A development like this would not be without its problems. Such councils might be even more socially unrepresentative than present ones if it was found necessary to exclude employees of all public authorities from elected membership. This could be overcome by some device equivalent to a strict declaration of interest or by restricting such councillors to areas of business other than that dealing with their employers. If the councils were to be more than mere talking shops they would need to possess more sanctions than those of exposure and publicity. Perhaps they would have to develop direct access to an enlarged ombudsman system. The present arrangements for ombudsmen for local government and the health service might be combined and expanded. If this were done along the lines of the Commissioner of Complaints for Northern Ireland, it would provide an ombudsman service that covered local government, public corporations and the health service, and which was charged not merely with producing reports on complaints but also with effecting a settlement of disputes wherever possible (Elcock, 1972). Whether the terms of reference of such an ombudsman could or should extend beyond the present limits of complaints involving maladministration is an open question.

The Central Problem

The three possible developments outlined above represent different responses to the central problem of contemporary local politics. The problem is that of the ability of elected representatives, both individually and as party politicians, to cope with the pressures on their role which arise from the increasing technical expertise of the officials and the demand for greater participation by the public.

In the case of the first development — the councillor as figure-head — the local politician in effect abdicates and allows official expertise and public opinion to reach their own accommodation with each other. Such a development however opens the way for officers to bring their considerable resources of knowledge and expertise directly to bear on a public ill-equipped for an equal contest in the event of disagreement. It could become a recipe for the emergence of local professional 'baronies' each with their own captive followers amongst the public.

The second development — the councillor in control — represents an attempt by the councillors to reclaim control of the bureaucracy, and to use the machinery of the political parties to strengthen both their ties with public opinion and their ability to formulate policy effectively. It may solve the problem of the councillor's role, but not necessarily that of his accountability, unless it leads to such vigorous and explicit political debate on local policy making that local elections become verdicts on councillors rather than on the national government of the day.

The third development — the Council as consumers' forum — abandons any notions of prior authorisation through public participation, and any idea of the councillor as policy maker. Instead it sees the councillor as a social auditor, evaluating policy outcomes in terms of consumer response over a wide range of public services. It emphasises accountability after the event. Admittedly it provides no formal

sanctions by which changes in unsatisfactory policies can be ensured,
since the councillors have no direct power over the various officials
who make the policy decisions in the different public bodies.
Nevertheless, the presence of a permanent body of elected and
informed public critics would certainly alter the local political climate
in which these officials took their decisions.

It is tempting to argue that perhaps one solution to the central
problem would be found by adopting elements of each of the three
developments into a fourth composite development. From the idea of
the councillor as figure-head could be adopted the practice of greater use
of market research techniques as participatory devices, if necessary
replacing exhibitions, brochures, public meetings and evenings spent
closeted with active members of local societies. From the notion of the
councillor in control could be taken the idea of perhaps a small number
of full-time councillors of quasi-ministerial status backed by effective
local parties. From the consumers' forum development could be taken
the idea of a separate body of councillors concerned solely with
consumer response. Instead of looking for solutions through governmental
devolution, with an ultimate structure of region, county, district and
neighbourhood parish or community councils, this would herald a move
towards balancing government by 'counter-government'. It means
separating out the statesmen and the tribunes, and externalising the
internal dialogue between makers and reviewers of policy which was
suggested by Maud. By giving both independence and resources to critics
of local policy it might invigorate local politics and perhaps put local
issues back on the agenda at local elections.

This composite development might go some way towards enabling
representative democracy and public participation to co-exist at the
local level, and would ensure that technical expertise and resources
were at the command of politicians and public critics instead of being
the exclusive preserve of local officials. It would be pleasant to
recommend such a development as a sure way out of the present
dilemmas of local government. But honesty requires a note of caution.

To believe that such reforms of institutions and procedures can in
themselves solve the problem would be to take too narrow a view of
local government and its politics. Blueprints for a better local politics
should not ignore the wider social situation. The problems of
contemporary local democracy are not unique. It may be that they
are clearly evident because of their more direct and observable impact
on the public at large. But it is possible that they are merely symptomatic
of a more widespread condition. Daniel Bell has argued that throughout

Western post-industrial society a major source of tension and conflict lies in the co-existence of a desire for greater participation in decision making with an increasing technical complexity in the decision making process itself. Thus whilst 'the participation revolution is one of the forms of reaction against the professionalisation of society and. . .technocratic decision making' this reaction should not be allowed to hide the fact that 'the politician, and the political public, will have to become increasingly versed in the technical character of policy. . .'. Bell concludes that 'the relationship of technical and political decisions in the next decades will become. . .one of the most crucial problems of public policy' (Bell, 1973, pp.364-5). If this insight has any value at all then it suggests very clearly that the problems outlined in this book, of relating expertise, representation and participation at the local level, are ultimately not problems peculiar to local government, but are intrinsic to politics at all levels of society.

SOURCES

1. Bibliography

Adrian, C.R. (1952), 'General characteristics of non-partisan elections', *American Political Science Review,* vol.46, no.3, pp.766-76.

Alt, J. (1971), 'Some social and political correlates of county borough expenditures', *British Journal of Political Science,* vol.1, no.1, pp.49-62.

Amos, F.J.C. (1973), 'Liverpool', in Holliday, J. (ed.), *City Centre Redevelopment* (London, Charles Knight and Co.).'

Arnstein, S.R. (1971), 'A Ladder of Citizen Participation in the U.S.A.', *Journal of the Royal Town Planning Institute,* vol.57, no.4, pp.176-82.

Aronson, J.R. (1974), 'Voting with your feet', *New Society,* 20 August.

Ashford, D.E. (1974), 'The Effects of Central Finance on the British Local Government System', *British Journal of Political Science,* vol.4, no.3, pp.305-22.

Aves, G.M. (1969), *The Voluntary Worker in the Social Services* (London, Allen and Unwin).

Balfe, R. (1972), 'Labour's List', *New Society,* 1 June.

Banfield, E. (1972), 'Urban Renewal and the Planners', *Policy and Politics,* vol. 1, no. 2, pp.163-9.

—— , and Wilson, J.Q. (1963), *City Politics* (Cambridge, Mass., Harvard University Press).

Banwell, H. (1963), 'The Machinery of Local Government: the Creaks', *Public Administration,* vol.41, pp.335-45.

Barker, A. (1972), 'Communities' and 'Normal Politics', *Government and Opposition,* vol.7, no.2, pp.153-65.

——, and Rush M. (1970), *The Member of Parliament and his Information* (London, Allen and Unwin).

Barker, S. (1968), 'Selecting Local Government Candidates', *Labour Organiser,* November.

Barratt, C. (1963), 'The Town Clerk in British Local Government', *Public Administration,* vol.41, pp.152-72.

Barry, B. (1974), 'Size and Democracy', *Government and Opposition,* vol.9, no.4, pp.492-503.

Batley, R. (1972), 'An Explanation of Non-Participation in Planning', *Policy and Politics,* vol.1, no.2, pp.95-114.

Baxter, R. (1972), 'The Working Class and Labour Politics', *Political*

Studies, vol.20, no.1, pp.97-107.

Bealey, F.J., Blondel, J., and McCann, W.P. (1965), *Constituency Politics* (London, Faber).

Beith, A. (1965), 'The Council and the Press', *New Society,* 9 September.

────── (1973), 'An Anti-Labour Caucus: the Case of the Northumberland Voters Association', *Policy and Politics,* vol.2, no.2, pp.153-65.

Bell, D. (1973), *The Coming of Post-Industrial Society* (New York, Basic Books).

────── , and Held, V. 1969, 'The Community Revolution', *Public Interest,* no.16, pp.142-77.

Benham, H. (1964), *Two Cheers for the Town Hall* (London, Hutchinson).

Benn, C. (1974), 'Education in Committee', *New Society,* 28 February.

Bentley, S. (1972), 'Intergroup relations in local politics: Pakistanis and Bangladeshis', *New Community,* vol.2, no.1, pp.44-8.

Berkshire, T. (1974), 'Devising a System of Measurement in a Metropolitan Authority', *Local Government Studies,* no.7, pp.39-52.

Berry, D. (1969), 'Party Membership and Social Participation', *Political Studies,* vol.17, no.2, pp.196-207.

────── (1970), *The Sociology of Grass-Roots Politics* (London, Macmillan).

Bilski, R. (1973), 'Ideology and the Comprehensive School', *Political Quarterly,* vol.44, pp.197-211.

Binns, I. (1973), 'What are we trying to achieve through community action?', *Community Action,* no.6, pp.12-13.

Birch, A.H. (1959), *Small-town Politics* (London, Oxford University Press).

Blaydon, S. (1974), 'Corporate Planning – can the councillor take control', *Municipal Review,* no.534, pp.90-2.

Blondel, J. (1958), 'The Conservative Association and the Labour Party in Reading', *Political Studies,* vol.6, no.2, pp.101-19.

────── and Hall, R. (1967), 'Conflict, Decisionmaking, and the Perceptions of Local Councillors', *Political Studies,* vol.15, no.3, pp.322-50.

Boaden, N.T. (1969), 'Local Elections and Party Policies', *New Society,* 8 May.

────── (1970), 'Central Departments and Local Authorities: The Relationship Examined', *Political Studies,* vol.18, no.2, pp.175-86.

────── (1971a), 'Innovation and Change in English Local Government, *Political Studies,* vol.19, no.4, pp.416-29.

────── (1971b), *Urban Policy-Making* (London, Cambridge University

Press).

—— and Alford, R.R. (1969), 'Sources of Diversity in English Local Government Decisions', *Public Administration,* vol.47, pp.203-24.

Bochel, J.M. (1966), 'The Recruitment of Local Councillors: A Case Study', *Political Studies,* vol.14, no.3, pp.360-4.

——, and Denver, D.T. (1971), 'Canvassing, turnout, and party support: an experiment', *British Journal of Political Science,* vol.1, no.3, pp.257-69.

——, and Denver, D.T. (1972), 'The impact of the campaign on the results of local government elections', *British Journal of Political Science,* vol.2, no.2, pp.239-44.

——, and Denver, D.T. (1973), 'Politics.in the City', in Urban Development Course Team, *The System of Control* (Milton Keynes, Open University).

Bonnor, J. (1954), 'Public Interest in Local Government', *Public Administration,* vol.54, pp.425-8.

Boyle, E., Playfair, E., Keith-Lucas, B., Darlow, G.F., and Johnson, N. (1965), 'Who are the Policy Makers?', *Public Administration,* vol.43, pp.251-88.

Boyle, E., and Crosland, C.A.R. (1971), *The Politics of Education* (Harmondsworth, Penguin).

Brabin, H. ('Special Correspondent') (1961), 'The Party System in Local Government', *The Councillor,* vol.4, no.7, pp.8-12.

Brand, J.A. (1965), 'Ministry Control and local autonomy in education', *Political Quarterly,* vol.36, pp.154-63.

—— (1971), 'The Politics of Fluoridation: A Community Conflict', *Political Studies,* vol.19, no.4, pp.430-9.

—— (1973), 'Party Organisation and the Recruitment of Councillors', *British Journal of Political Science,* vol.3, no.4, pp.473-86.

—— (1974), *Local Government Reform in England* (London, Croom Helm).

—— (1974), 'Policy Making: keeping the politicians in control', *Municipal Review,* no.536, pp.142-3.

Bredin, J. (1970), 'Television for local communities', in Weddell, E. (ed.), *Structures of Broadcasting* (Manchester, Manchester University Press).

Brennan, T., Cooney, E.W., and Pollins, H. (1954), Party Politics and local Government in Western South Wales', *Political Quarterly,* vol.25, pp.76-83.

Brier, A.P. (1970), 'The Decision Process in Local Government: A Case Study of Fluoridization in Hull', *Public Administration,* vol.48, pp.153-68.

—, and Dowse, R.E. (1969), 'The Politics of the A-political', *Political Studies,* vol.17, no.3, pp.334-9.

Briggs, A. (1968), *Victorian Cities* (Harmondsworth, Penguin).

Brill, M. (1974), 'The local authority social worker', in Jones, K. (ed.), *The Year Book of Social Policy in Britain, 1973* (London, Routledge), pp.81-97.

Bristow, S.L. (1972), 'The Criteria for Local Government Reorganisation and Local Authority Autonomy', *Policy and Politics,* vol.1, no.2, pp.143-62.

— (1975), 'Women in County Government', *County Councils Gazette,* vol.68, no.1, pp.10-11.

British Association of Social Workers (1973), *Social Services: the Councillor's Task* (London, B.A.S.W.).

Brooke, H. (1953), 'Conservatives and Local Government', *Political Quarterly,* vol.24, pp.181-9.

Brown, J.C. (1958), 'Local Party Efficiency as a factor in the outcome of British Elections', *Political Studies,* vol.6, no.2, pp.174-8.

Brown, J.F. (1972), 'Some Social and Political Correlates of County Borough Expenditures – a comment' (with rejoinder by Alt, J.E.), *British Journal of Political Science,* vol.2, no.1, pp.131-2.

Brown, K. (1970), 'Radio for Local Communities – a manager's view', in E.G. Weddell (ed.), *Structures of Broadcasting* (Manchester, Manchester University Press).

Brown, T., Vile, M.J.C., and Whitemore, M.F. (1972), 'Community Studies and Decision-taking', *British Journal of Political Science,* vol.2, no.2, pp.133-53.

Bryant, R. (1972), 'Community Action', *British Journal of Social Work,* vol.2, no.2, pp.205-15.

— (1974), 'Linking Community and Industrial Action', *Community Development Journal,* vol.9, no.1, pp.28-32.

Budge, I. (1965), 'Electors' Attitudes towards Local Government: A Survey of a Glasgow Constituency', *Political Studies,* vol.13, no.4, pp.386-92.

—, Brand, J.A., Margolis, M. and Smith, A.L.M., (1972), *Political Stratification and Democracy* (London, Macmillan).

—, and Farlie, D. (1975), 'Political Recruitment and Dropout: Predictive Success of Background Characteristics over Five British Localities', *British Journal of Political Science,* vol.5, no.1, pp.33-68.

Bulpitt, J.G. (1963), 'Party Systems in Local Government', *Political Studies,* vol.11, no.1, pp.11-35.

—— (1967), *Party Politics in English Local Government* (London, Longmans).

—— (1968), 'Are Local Elections Important?', *New Society,* 9 May.

—— (1972), 'Participation and Local Government: Territorial Democracy', in G. Party (ed.), *Participation in Politics* (Manchester, Manchester University Press).

Burke, R. (1970), *The Murky Cloak: Local Authority Press Relations* (London, Charles Knight).

Butler D., and Stokes D. (1975), *Political Change in Britain* (London, Macmillan).

Butterworth, R. (1966), 'Islington Borough Council: Some Characteristics of Single-party Rule', *Politics,* vol.1, no.1, pp.21-31.

Buxton, R. (1973), *Local Government* (Harmondsworth, Penguin).

Calmfors, H. (1972), 'Remuneration of Local Government Representatives in Sweden', *Local Government Studies,* no.3, pp.63-74.

Cartwright, J. (1974), 'Corporate Planning and the Elected Member', *London Review of Public Administration,* no.5, pp.2-11.

Castles, F.G. (1967), *Pressure Groups and Political Culture* (London, Routledge).

Cheetham, J., and Hill, M. (1973), 'Community Work: Social Realities and Ethical Dilemmas', *British Journal of Social Work,* vol. 3, pp.331-48.

Chester, D.N. (1954), 'Council and Committee Meetings in County Boroughs', *Public Administration,* vol.32, pp.429-31.

—— (1968), 'Local Democracy and the Internal Organisation of Local Authorities', *Public Administration,* vol.46, pp.287-98.

Chipperfield, G.H. (1964), 'The City Manager and Chief Administrative Officer', *Public Administration,* vol.42, pp.123-32.

Chitnis, P. (ed.) (1960), *Local Government Handbook* (London, Liberal Publications Department).

Churchill, R. (1959), *Lord Derby: King of Lancashire* (London, Heinemann).

Clarke, M.G. (1969), 'National Organisation and the Constituency Association in the Conservative Party: the case of the Huddersfield Pact', *Political Studies,* vol.17, no.3, pp.343-7.

Clarke, P.F. (1971), *Lancashire and the New Liberalism* (London, Cambridge University Press).

Clements, R.V. (1969), *Local Notables and the City Council* (London, Macmillan).

Coates, K., and Silburn, R. (1970), *Poverty: the forgotten Englishmen*

(Harmondsworth, Penguin).

Cockburn, C. (1970), *Opinion and Planning Education* (London, Centre for Environmental Studies).

Cohen, L.H. (1973), 'Local Government Complaints: the MP's viewpoint', *Public Administration,* vol.51, pp.175-83.

Cole, G.D.H. (1947), *Local and Regional Government* (London, Cassell).

—— (1948), *A History of the Labour Party from 1914* (London, Routledge).

Cole, M. (1956), *Servant of the County* (London, Dobson Books).

Collins, A. (1944), 'The Expert in the Local Government Service', *Public Administration,* vol.22, pp.40-6.

Collison, P. (1963), *The Cutteslowe Walls* (London, Faber & Faber).

Committee on Local Authority and Allied Personal Social Services (1968), *Report* (London, HMSO).

Committee on the Management of Local Government (1967), (London, HMSO).

Volume 1. *Report;*

Volume 2. *The Local Government Councillor;*

Volume 3. *The Local Government Elector;*

Volume 4. *Local Government Administration Abroad;*

Volume 5. *Local Government Administration in England and Wales.*

Conservative Party (1958), 'Local Government Department', *Report of Annual Conference of the Conservative and Unionist Party, 1958.*

Conservative Party (1971), *Local Government and the Party Organisation* (London, Conservative Central Office).

Consumer Council (1968), *Consumer Consultative Machinery in the Nationalised Industries* (London, HMSO).

Cook, C. (1975), 'Liberals, Labour and Local Elections', in G. Peele and C. Cook (eds.), *The Politics of Reappraisal 1918-1939* (London, Macmillan).

Cooper, S. (1974), 'Planning Advice Centres', *Municipal Journal,* 14 June.

Corina, L. (1974), 'Elected Representatives in a Party System: A Typology', *Policy and Politics,* vol.3, no.1, pp.69-87.

Cossey, C. (1974), *Building Better Communities,* Fabian Tract 429 (London, Fabian Society).

Cousins, P.F. (1973a & b), 'Voluntary Organisations as Pressure Groups', *London Review of Public Administration,* no.3, pp.22-30 and no.4, pp.17-26.

Cox, H., and Morgan, D. (1973), *City Politics and the Press* (London, Cambridge University Press).

Craig, F.W.S. (1974), *Greater London Votes: The Greater London Council 1964-70* (London, Macmillan).

Crockett, D.G. (1967), 'The M.P. and his Constituents', *Parliamentary Affairs,* vol.20, pp.281-4.

Cross, C.A. (1974), *Principles of Local Government Law* (London, Sweet & Maxwell).

Davies, B. (1968), *Social Needs and Resources in Local Services* (London, Michael Joseph).

—— (1969), 'Welfare Departments and Territorial Justice', *Social and Economic Administration,* vol.3, no.4, pp.233-52.

—— (1972), *Variations in Children's Services among British Urban Authorities: A Causal Analysis* (London, Bell).

——, Barton, A., McMillan, I., and Williamson, V. (1971), *Variations in Services for the Aged: A Causal Analysis* (London, Bell).

Davies, C.J. (1970), 'Comparative Local Government as a field of study', *Studies in Comparative Local Government,* vol.4, no.2, pp.38-44.

Davies, J.C. (1966), *Neighbourhood Groups and Urban Renewal* (New York, Columbia University Press).

Davies, J.G. (1972a), *The Evangelistic Bureaucrat* (London, Tavistock).

—— (1972b), 'The Local Councillor's Dilemma', *Official Architecture and Planning,* February, pp.112-14.

Deacon, A., and Briggs, E. (1974), 'Local Democracy and Central Policy: the Issue of Pauper Votes in the 1920's', *Policy and Politics,* vol.2, no.4, pp.347-64.

Dearlove, J. (1971), 'Councillors and Interest Groups in Kensington and Chelsea', *British Journal of Political Science,* vol.1, no.2, pp.129-53.

—— (1973), *The Politics of Policy in Local Government* (London, Cambridge University Press).

Dell, E. (1960), 'Labour and Local Government', *Political Quarterly,* vol.31, pp.333-47.

Dennis, N. (1958), 'The Popularity of the Neighbourhood Community Ideal', in Pahl, R. (ed.) (1968), *Readings in Urban Sociology* (Oxford, Pergamon).

—— (1972a), *Public Participation and Planner's Blight* (London, Faber and Faber).

—— (1972b), 'Who Governs?', *Community Action,* pp.34-5.

Denver, D.T., and Hands, G. (1972), 'Turnout and marginality in local elections: a comment' (with a rejoinder by Newton, K.), *British Journal of Political Science,* vol.2, no.4, pp.513-16.

Department of the Environment (1972a), *Fifty Million Volunteers* (London, HMSO).
—— (1972b), *The New Local Authorities: management and structure* (London, HMSO).
—— (1974), *Local Ombudsman* (London, HMSO).
Dinnage, R. (1972), 'Parliamentary Advice Bureau', *New Society*, 24 February.
Dixey, R. (1974), 'Halstead: A case study in local enterprise', *Public Enterprise*, no.7, pp.15-16.
Donnison, D.V. (1962), *Health, Welfare and Democracy in Greater London*, Greater London Paper 5 (London, London School of Economics and Political Science).
—— (1970), 'Government and Governed', *New Society*, 5 March.
—— (1973), 'Micro-politics of the City', in D.V. Donnison and D. Eversley (eds.), *London: Urban Patterns, Problems and Policies* (London, Heinemann).
——, and Plowman, D.E.G. (1954), 'The Functions of Local Labour Parties', *Political Studies*, vol.2, no.2, pp.154-67.
Donnison, D. *et al.* (1965), *Social Policy and Administration* (London, Allen and Unwin).
Donoughue, B., and Jones, E.W. (1973), *Herbert Morrison, Portrait of a Politician* (London, Weidenfeld and Nicolson).
Dowse, R.E. (1963), 'The M.P. and his Surgery', *Political Studies*, vol.11, no.4, pp.333-41.
Drake, C.D. (1970), 'Ombudsman for Local Government', *Public Administration*, vol.48, pp.179-89.
Drummond, S. (1962), 'The Election of the First Durham County Council', *Public Administration*, vol.40, pp.141-50.
Dunrabin, J.P.O. (1963), 'The Politics of the Establishment of County Councils', *Historical Journal*, vol.6, pp.226-52.
—— (1965), 'Expectations of the new County Councils and their realisation', *Historical Journal*, vol. 8, pp.353-79.
Dunsire, A. (1956), 'Accountability in Local Government', *Administration*, vol.4, no.3, pp.80-8.
Eggleston, S.J. (1966), 'Going Comprehensive', *New Society*, 22 December.
Elcock, H.J. (1972), 'Opportunity for Ombudsman: The Northern Ireland Commission for Complaints', *Public Administration*, vol.50, pp.87-93.
Elkin, S.L. (1974a), *Politics and Land Use Planning* (London, Cambridge University Press).

—— (1974b), 'Comparative Urban Politics and Interorganisational Behaviour', *Policy and Politics,* vol.2, no.4, pp.289-303.

Elliott, J. (1971), 'The Harris Experiment in Newcastle upon Tyne', *Public Administration,* vol.49, pp.149-62.

Ensor, P. (1975), 'What the Other Papers Say', *Guardian,* 7 April.

Epstein, L.D. (1960), 'British M.P.'s and Their Local Parties: The Suez Cases', *American Political Science Review,* vol.54, no.2, pp.374-90.

Eulau, H., Wahlke, J.C., Buchanan, W., and Ferguson, L.C. (1959), 'The Role of the Representative: Some Empirical Observations on the Theory of Edmund Burke', *American Political Science Review,* vol.53, no.3, pp.742-56.

Evening Standard (1975), 'No Case', an editorial, 12 March.

Eversley, D. (1973), *The Planner in Society* (London, Faber & Faber).

Fletcher, P. (1969), 'An Explanation of Variations in Turnout in Local Elections', *Political Studies,* vol.17, no.4.

Forrester, T. (1973), 'Anatomy of a Local Labour Party', *New Statesman,* 28 September and 5 October.

Foster, J. (1974), *Class Struggle and the Industrial Revolution* (London, Weidenfeld & Nicolson).

Fraser, D. (1973), 'Areas of Urban Politics: Leeds 1830-80', in H.J. Dyos, and M. Wolff (eds.), *The Victorian City* (London, Routledge).

French, C.A. (1962), 'Public Board and Local Authority: Some reflections on their administration', *Public Administration,* vol.40, pp.245-52.

Friedrich, C. (1937), *Constitutional Government and Democracy,* (New York, Harper).

Friend, J.K., and Jessop, W.N. (1969), *Local Government and Strategic Choice* (London, Tavistock).

Gans, H. (1972), *People and Plans* (Hammondsworth, Penguin).

Gash, N. (1953), *Politics in the Age of Peel* (London, Longmans).

Glassberg, A. (1973), 'The Linkage between Urban Policy Outputs and Voting Behaviour — New York and London', *British Journal of Political Science,* vol.3, no.3, pp.341-62.

Glastonbury, B., Burdett, M., and Austin, R. (1973), 'Community Perceptions and the Social Services', *Policy and Politics,* vol.1, no.3, pp.191-211.

G.L.C. (1974), *London Borough Council Elections — 2 May, 1974,* (London, Greater London Council)

Glennerster, H., and Hatch, S. (eds.) (1974), *Positive Discrimination and Inequality,* Fabian Research Series 314 (London, Fabian Society).

Grainger, J.H. (1959), 'Local Community and Local Government', *The Listener,* 10 December.

Grant, W.P. (1970), 'The Implications of Radcliffe-Maud for Local Interest Groups', *South Western Review of Public Administration,* no.8, pp.23-7.

—— (1971a), 'Attitudes towards Local Government in a Small Resort Town', *South Western Review of Public Administration,* no.10, pp.34-9.

—— (1971b), 'Local Councils, Conflict and "Rules of the Game"', *British Journal of Political Science,* vol.1, no.2, pp.253-6.

—— (1971c), '"Local Parties" in British Local Politics: A Framework for Empirical Analysis', *Political Studies,* vol.19, no.2, pp.201-12.

—— (1972), 'Size of place and local Labour strength', *British Journal of Political Science,* vol.2, no.2, pp.259-69.

—— (1973), 'Non-partisanship in British Local Politics', *Policy and Politics,* vol.1, no.3, pp.241-66.

Grayson, L. (1974a), 'Information services for the GLC elected member', *Greater London Intelligence Quarterly,* no.27, pp.5-9.

—— (1974b), 'Members Information Services', *Greater London Intelligence Quarterly,* no.28, pp.41-4.

Green, G. (1972), 'National, city and ward components of local voting', *Policy and Politics,* vol.1, no.1, pp.45-54.

—— (1974), 'Politics, Local Government and the Community', *Local Government Studies,* no.8, pp.5-16.

Green, L.P. (1959), *Provisional Metropolis* (London, Allen and Unwin).

Greene, H.C. (1961), 'Local Broadcasting and the Local Authority', *Public Administration,* vol.39, pp.323-30.

Greenwood, R., Norton, A.L., and Stewart, J.D. (1969), 'Recent Changes in the Internal Organisation of County Boroughs', *Public Administration,* vol.47, pp.151-68 and 289-306.

——, Stewart, J.D., and Smith, A.D. (1972), 'The Policy Committee in English Local Government', *Public Administration,* vol.50, pp.157-66.

——, and Stewart, J.D. (1972), 'Corporate Planning and Management Organisation', *Local Government Studies,* no.3, pp.25-40.

——, and Stewart, J.D. (1973), 'Towards a Typology of English Local Authorities', *Political Studies,* vol.21, no.1, pp.64-9.

——, Hinings, C.R., and Ranson, P.R.S. (1974), 'Inside the local authorities', in K. Jones (ed.), *The Year Book of Social Policy in Britain, 1973* (London, Routledge), pp.34-47.

Gregory, R. (1969), 'Local Elections and the "Rule of Anticipated Reactions"', *Political Studies,* vol.17, no.1, pp.31-47.

Griffith, J.A.G. (1950), 'The Voice of the Consumer', *Political Quarterly*, vol.XXI, no.2, April-June, pp.177-83.

—— (1965), 'Local Democracy: a Sorry State?', *New Society*, 14 February.

—— (1966), 'The Traditional Pattern Reconsidered', *Political Quarterly*, vol.33, pp.139-48.

—— (1969), 'Maud – Off the Target', *New Statesman*, 20 June.

—— (1974), 'Public Faces and Private Conduct', *New Statesman*, 31 May.

Griffiths, H. (1974), 'The Aims and Objectives of Community Development', *Community Development Journal*, vol.9, no.2, pp.88-95.

Grimond, J. (1972), 'Community Politics', *Government and Opposition*, vol.7, no.2, pp.135-44.

Groombridge, B. (1972), *Television and the People* (Harmondsworth, Penguin).

Grundy, J. (1950), 'Non-voting in an urban district', *Manchester School of Economic and Social Studies*, vol.18, pp.83-99.

Gunlicks, A.B. (1969), 'Representative Role Perceptions among Local Councillors in Western Germany', *Journal of Politics*, vol.31, no.2, pp.443-64.

Hall, C. (1974), *How to Run a Pressure Group* (London, J.M. Dent).

Hampton, W. (1966), 'The County as a Political Unit', *Parliamentary Affairs*, vol.19, pp.462-74.

—— (1968), 'The Electoral Response to a Multi-Vote Ballot', *Political Studies*, vol.16, no.2, pp.266-72.

—— (1969), 'Local Government and Community', *Political Quarterly*, vol.40, pp.151-62.

—— (1970), *Democracy and Community* (London, Oxford University Press).

—— (1971), 'Democratic Planning', *Parliamentary Affairs*, vol.24, pp.338-46.

—— (1972a), 'Local Authorities and the Making of Social Policy', *Political Studies*, vol.20, no.2, pp.222-5.

—— (1972b), 'Political Attitudes to changes in City Council Administration', *Local Government Studies*, no.2, pp.23-35.

—— (1973), 'Divided Cities', *Political Studies*, vol.21, no.2, pp.219-23.

——, and Chapman, J.J. (1971), 'Towards Neighbourhood Councils', *Political Quarterly*, vol.42, pp.245-54 and 414-22.

Hang, M.R., and Sussman, M.O. (1969), 'Professional Autonomy and the Revolt of the Client', *Social Problems*, vol.17, no.2, pp.153-61.

Hanham, H.J. (1956), 'The Local Organisation of the British Labour Party', *Western Political Quarterly*, vol.9, pp.376, 388.
—— (1959), *Elections and Party Management* (London, Longmans).
—— (1966), 'Opposition techniques in British Politics, 1967-1914'. *Government and Opposition*, vol.2, no.1, pp.25-48.
—— (1971), 'The First Constituency Party?', *Political Studies*, vol.9, no.2, pp.188-9.
Hare, D.M. (1974), 'The Need for New Anti-Corruption Laws in Local Government', *Public Law*, pp. 146-74.
Harrington, I. (1971), 'Young Turks of the Town Halls', *New Statesman*, 16 July.
Harrison, P. (1973), 'The Neighbourhood Council', *New Society*, 12 April.
Hartley, O. (1971), 'The Relationship between Central Government and Local Authorities', *Public Administration*, vol.49, pp.439-56.
—— (1973), 'The Functions of Local Government', *Local Government Studies*, no.4, pp.27-40.
Harvey, D. (1973), *Social Justice and the City* (London, Arnold).
Hasluck, E.L. (1948), *Local Government in England*, 2nd edition (London, Cambridge University Press).
Hatch, S. (ed.) (1973), *Towards Participation in Local Services*, Fabian Tract 419 (London, Fabian Society).
Headrick, T.E. (1962), *The Town Clerk in English Local Government* (London, Allen & Unwin).
Heclo, H.H. (1969), 'The Councillor's Job', *Public Administration*, vol.47, pp.185-202.
Hennock, E.P. (1963), 'Finance and Politics in urban local government in England 1835-1900', *Historical Journal*, vol.6, pp.212-25.
—— (1973), *Fit and Proper Persons: Ideal and Reality in 19th century urban government* (London, Edward Arnold).
Herrick, F. (1945), 'The Origins of the National Liberal Federation', *Journal of Modern History*, vol.17, no.2, pp.116-29.
Higgins, G.M., and Richardson, J.J. (1971), 'Local Government and Public Participation: a Case Study', *Local Government Studies*, no.1, pp.19-31.
Hill, D.M. (1965), 'Local Authorities and the Press', *Local Government Chronicle*, 4 and 11 December.
—— (1970), *Participating in Local Affairs* (Harmondsworth, Penguin).
—— (1974), *Democratic Theory and Local Government* (London, Allen and Unwin).
Hill, M.J. (1972), *The Sociology of Public Administration* (London,

Weidenfeld and Nicolson).

Hindess, B. (1967), 'Local Elections and the Labour Vote in Liverpool', *Sociology*, vol.1, no.2, pp.187-95.

—— (1971), *The Decline of Working Class Politics* (London, Granada Publishing).

Hinings, C.R., Ranson, P.R.S., and Greenwood, R. (1974), 'The Organisation of Metropolitan Government: The Impact of Bains', *Local Government Studies*, no.9, pp.47-54.

Hobson, M., and Stewart, J.D. (1969), 'The Legal Profession in Local Government', *Public Law*, pp.199-218.

Hodgkinson, G. (1970), *Sent to Coventry* (London, Robert Maxwell).

Hoffman, J.D. (1964), *The Conservative Party in Opposition* (London, McGibbon & Kee).

Holgate, S. (1970), 'Radio for local communities: a chairman's view', in E.G. Weddell (ed.), *Structures of Broadcasting* (Manchester, Manchester University Press).

Holman, R., and Hamilton, L. (1973), 'The British Urban Programme', *Policy and Politics*, vol.2, no.2, pp.97-112.

Holtham, C. (1973), 'Information Systems in Local Government', *Local Government Studies*, no.6, pp.45-57.

Homans, G.C. (1951), *The Human Group* (London, Routledge).

Hurley, C.W. (1971), 'The New Towns of Northumberland', *Studies in Comparative Local Government*, vol.5, no.1, pp.51-6.

Isaac-Henry, K. (1972), 'Policy processes in Local Government: a case study', *South Western Review of Public Administration*, no.11, pp.29-37.

IULA (1971), 'Citizen Participation and Local Government in Europe and the United States', *Studies in Comparative Local Government*, vol.5, no.2, pp.9-97.

Jackson, I. (1971), *The Provincial Press and the Community* (Manchester, Manchester University Press).

Jackson, R.M. (1965), *The Machinery of Local Government* (London, Macmillan).

James, R. (1973), 'Is there a case for Local Authority Policy Planning?' *Public Administration*, vol.51, pp.147-63.

Janosik, E.G. (1968), *Constituency Labour Parties in Britain* (London, Pall Mall Press).

Jay, A. (1972), *The Householders' Guide to Community Defence against Bureaucratic Aggression* (London, Jonathan Cape).

Jenkins, S. (1973a), 'The Press as Politician in Local Planning', *Political Quarterly*, vol.44, pp.47-57.

—— (1973b), 'The Politics of London Motorways', *Political Quarterly,* vol.244, pp.257-70.

Johnson, N. (1974), 'Defining Accountability', *Public Administration Bulletin,* no.17, December, pp.3-13.

Johnson, R.W. (1972), 'The Nationalisation of English Rural Politics: Norfolk South-West 1945-1970', *Parliamentary Affairs,* vol.26, pp.8-55.

Jones, G.W. (1969), *Borough Politics* (London, Macmillan).

—— (1973a), 'The Functions and Organisation of Councillors', *Public Administration,* vol.51, pp.135-46.

—— (1973b), 'The Local Government Act 1972 and the Redcliffe-Maud Commission', *Political Quarterly,* vol.44, pp.154-66.

—— (1973c), 'Political Leadership in Local Government: How Herbert Morrison Governed London, 1934-40', *Local Government Studies,* no.5, pp.1-11.

—— (1973d), 'Herbert Morrison and Poplarism', *Public Law,* pp.11-31.

Jupp, J. (1968), *Political Parties* (London, Routledge).

Kantor, P. (1974), 'The Governable City: Islands of Power and Political Parties in London', *Polity,* vol.7, no.1, pp.4-31.

Karplan, H. (1963), *Urban Renewal Politics* (New York, Columbia University Press).

Kavanagh, D. (1967), 'The Orientations of Community Leaders to Parliamentary Candidates', *Political Studies,* vol.15, no.3, pp.351-6.

—— (1970), *Constituency Electioneering in Britain* (London, Longmans).

Keast, H. (1974), 'Committee Structures in the Counties', *Local Government Chronicle,* 23 August.

Keith-Lucas, B. (1952), *The English Local Government Franchise* (Oxford, Basil Blackwell).

—— (1955), 'Local Government in Parliament', *Public Administration,* vol.33, pp.207-10.

—— (1961), *The Councils, the Press and the People* (London, Conservative Political Centre).

—— (1962), 'Poplarism', *Public Law,* pp.52-80.

Kellas, J.G. (1975), *The Scottish Political System* (London, Cambridge University Press).

Kimber, R., and Richardson, J.J. (1974), *Campaigning for the Environment* (London, Routledge).

Kinch, M.B. (1974), 'Departmental Reorganisation in a Local Authority', *Public Administration,* vol.52, pp.95-109.

King, D.N. (1973), 'Why do Local Authority Rate Poundages Differ?',

Public Administration, vol.51, no.2, pp.165-73.

Klein, R. (1973), 'Health Services: the case for a counter bureaucracy', in S. Hatch (ed.), *Towards Participation in Local Services,* Fabian Tract 419 (London, Fabian Society).

Knowles, R.S.B. (1971), *Modern Management in Local Government* (London, Butterworth).

Kogan, M. (with Van Der Eyken, W.) (1973), *County Hall: The Role of The Chief Education Officer* (Harmondsworth, Penguin).

Labour Party (1930), *Annual Conference Report* (London, The Labour Party).

—— (1973), *A Socialist Strategy for London: A GLC Election Manifesto* (Greater London Regional Council of the Labour Party).

—— (1975), *Rules (Sets A, B and C),* (London, Labour Party).

—— (n.d.), *Labour Groups on Local Authorities* (London, Labour Party).

Langrod, G. (1973), 'Local Government and Democracy', *Public Administration,* vol.31, pp.25-34.

Lapping, A. (ed.) (1970), *Community Action,* Fabian Tract 400 (London, Fabian Society).

Lee, J.M. (1963), *Social Leaders and Public Persons* (London, Oxford University Press).

——, Wood, B., Solomon, B.W., and Walters, P. (1974), *The Scope of Local Initiative* (London, Martin Robertson).

Lees, R. (1972), *Politics and Social Work* (London, Routledge).

Leonard, P. (1973), 'Professionalisation, Community Action, and the Growth of Social Service Bureaucracies', in P. Halmos (ed.), *Professionalisation and Social Change,* Sociological Review Monograph no.20, pp.103-17.

Leonard, R.L. (1968), 'Morrison's Political Bequest', *New Society,* 4 April.

Levin, P.H. (1973), 'Opening up the planning process', in S. Hatch (ed.), *Towards Participation in Local Services,* Fabian Tract 419 (London, Fabian Society).

Lipset, S.M. (1964), 'Introduction', in M. Ostrogorski, *Democracy and the Organisation of Political Parties* (New York, Anchor Books).

Lischeron, J., and Wall, T. (1974), 'Worker Participation', *Municipal Journal,* 10 May.

Lloyd, T. (1965), 'Uncontested Seats in British General Elections, 1852-1910', *Historical Journal,* vol.VIII, no.2, pp.260-5.

Lofts, D. (ed.) (1962), *Local Government Today. . .and Tomorrow* (London, Municipal Journal).

Lucking, R.C., Howard, F., and Greenwood, M. (1974), 'Corporate Planning and Management: A Review of their Application in English Local Government', *Town Planning Review,* vol.45, no.2, pp.131-45.

Lythgoe, J. (1949), 'The Administration of Services requiring local organisation', *Public Administration,* vol.27, pp.3-9.

Maccoll, J.E. (1949), 'The Party System in English Local Government', *Public Administration,* vol.27, pp.69-75.

McGill, B. (1962), 'Francis Schnadhorst and the Liberal Party Organisation', *Journal of Modern History,* vol.34, no.1, pp.19-39.

McHenry D.E. (1938), *The Labour Party in Transition 1931-1938,* (London, Routledge).

Mackenzie, W.J.M. (1951), 'Conventions of Local Government', *Public Administration,* vol.29, pp.345-56.

—— (1954), 'Local Government in Parliament', *Public Administration,* vol.32, pp.409-23.

McKie, D. (1973)' 'By-Elections of the Wilson Government', in C. Cook, and J. Ramsden (eds.) *By-Elections in British Politics* (London, Macmillan).

McKinsey and Co. (1973), *The Sunderland Study.* A report for the Department of the Environment (London, HMSO).

McKitterick, T.E.M. (1960), 'The Membership of the Party', *Political Quarterly,* vol.31, no.3, pp.312-23.

McLoughlin, B. (1973)' 'The Future of the Planning Profession', in P. Cowan (ed.), *The Future of Planning* (London, Heinemann).

Macrae, J. (1974), 'Brian Collins – enjoying the political atmosphere', *Municipal Engineering,* 17 May.

Maddick, H. (1966), 'The Local Government Service', *Political Quarterly,* vol.37, pp.192-205.

——, and Pritchard, E.P. (1959), 'Conventions of Local Authorities in the West Midlands', *Public Administration,* vol.36, pp.145-55, and vol.37, no.2, pp.135-43.

Madgwick, P., with Griffiths, N., and Walker V. (1973), *The Politics of Rural Wales* (London, Hutchinson).

May, J.D. (1973)' 'Opinion Structure of Political Parties: The Special Law of Curvilinear Disparity', *Political Studies,* vol.21, no.2, pp.135-51.

Mayer, J.E., and Timms, N. (1970), *The Client Speaks* (London. Routledge).

Meacher, M. (1971), 'Scrooge Areas', *New Society,* 2 December.

Mellors, C. (1974), 'Local Government in Parliament: Twenty Years Later', *Public Administration,* vol.52, pp.223-9.

Merton, R.K. (1957), 'Latent Functions of the Machine', in A.B. Callow

Jnr (ed.) (1966), *American Urban History* (New York, Oxford Univeristy Press).

Miller, D.C. (1958a), 'Industry and Community power structure: a comparative study of an American and an English City', *American Sociological Review,* vol.23, pp.9-15.

—— (1958b), 'Decision-making cliques in community power structures: a comparative study of an American and an English city', *American Journal of Sociology,* no.64, pp.299-310.

Miller, H. (1968), 'Value Dilemmas in Social Casework', *Social Work,* vol.13, no.1, pp.27-33.

Miner, J. (1973), 'British Local Expenditure Analysis: an American Evaluation', *Policy and Politics,* vol.1, no.4, pp.357-61.

Ministry of Housing and Local Government (1969), *People and Planning* (London, HMSO).

Minns, R. (1974), 'The Significance of Clay Cross: Another Look at District Audit', *Policy and Politics,* vol.2, no.4, pp.309-29.

Mitchell, A. (1974), 'Clay Cross', *Political Quarterly,* vol.45, pp.165-78.

Money, W.J. (1973), 'The Need to Sustain a Viable System of Local Democracy', *Urban Studies,* vol.10, no.3, pp.319-33.

Moodie, G.C., and Studdert-Kennedy, G. (1970), *Opinions, Public and Pressure Groups* (London, Allen and Unwin).

Morlan, R.L. (1964), 'Cabinet Government at the Municipal Level: the Dutch Experience', *Western Political Quarterly,* vol.17, pp.317-24.

Morris, A.J.A. (1969), 'Local Authority Relations with the Local Press', *Public Law,* pp.280-99.

Morris, D.S., and Newton, K. (1971a), 'Marginal Wards and Social Class', *British Journal of Political Science,* vol.1, no.4, pp.503-7.

——, and Newton, K. (1971b), 'The Social Composition of a City Council, 1925-1966', *Social and Economic Administration,* vol.5, no.1, pp.29-33.

Morton, J. (1970), 'Parish Pumps Revived', *New Society,* 29 January.

Moulin, L. (1954), 'Local Self-Government as a basis for democracy: a further comment', *Public Administration,* vol.32, pp.433-7.

Muchnik, D. (1970), *Urban Renewal in Liverpool* (London, Bell).

Mukhopadhyay, A.K. (1972), 'The Establishment of the Metropolitan Boroughs: A Note', *Public Administration,* vol.50, pp.207-11.

Murphy, D. (1974), 'The unfreedom of the local press', *New Society,* 19 December.

Musgrove, F. (1961), 'The Educational and Geographical Background of some Local Leaders', *British Journal of Sociology,* vol.1, no.4, pp.363-74.

NALGO (1957), 'Interest in Local Government', *Public Administration*, vol.35, pp.305-9.

National Opinion Polls (N.O.P.) (1973), 'G.L.C. Elections', *National Opinion Polls Bulletin*, April 1973 (Appendix).

—— (1975), 'Public Participation in Local Government', *Political Economic Social Review*, no.1, pp.17-34.

Newcastle City Council (1974), 'The Basis of a Social Contract for the City Council of Newcastle upon Tyne', *Joint Report of the Chief Executive and the City Personnel Officer to the Works Committee: 21 October.*

Newman, R. (1973), 'Communities and Local Authority Boundaries', *South Western Review of Public Administration*, Nos. 12-13 (double issue), pp.36-42.

Newton, K. (1969), 'City Politics in Britain and the United States', *Political Studies*, vol.17, no.2, pp.208-18.

—— (1972a), 'Democracy, Community Power and Non-Decision making', *Political Studies*, vol.20, no.4, pp.484-7.

—— (1972b), 'Turnout and marginality in local elections', *British Journal of Political Science*, vol.2, no.2, pp.251-5.

—— (1973), 'Links Between Leaders and Citizens in a Local Political System', *Policy and Politics*, vol.1, no.4, pp.287-305.

—— (1974a), 'Voluntary Organisations in community politics', *SSRC Newsletter*, no.24, pp.5-7.

—— (1974b), 'Role orientations and their sources among elected representatives in English local politics', *Journal of Politics*, vol.36, no.3, pp.614-36.

Newton, R. (1968), 'Society and Politics in Exeter, 1837-1914', in H.J. Dyos (ed.), *The Study of Urban History* (London, Edward Arnold).

Nicholson, R.H., and Topham, N. (1971), 'The determination of investment in housing by local authorities: an econometric approach' (with discussion), *Journal of the Royal Statistical Society*, vol.134, part 3, pp.273-320.

——, and Topham, N. (1972), 'Investment decisions and the size of local authorities', *Policy and Politics*, vol.1, no.1, pp.23-44.

Normanton, E.L. (1971), 'Public Accountability and Audit: A Reconaissance', in B.L.R. Smith and D.C. Hague (eds.), *The Dilemma of Accountability in Modern Government* (London, Macmillan).

Norton, A. (1972), 'Lessons from Reorganisation in the 1960s', *Local Government Studies*, no.3, pp.41-56.

——, and Stewart, J.D. (1973), 'Recommendations to the New Local

Authorities', *Local Government Studies,* no.6, pp.1-28.

Nottinghamshire Labour Party (1973), *The Way Ahead* (Nottingham).

Oliver, F.R., and Stanyer, J. (1969), 'Some Aspects of the Financial
   Behaviour of County Boroughs', *Public Administration,* vol.47,
   pp.169-84.

Ostrogorski, M. (1964), *Democracy and the Organisation of Political
   Parties* (New York, Doubleday).

Pahl, R.E. (1970), *Whose City?* (London, Longman's).

Palmer, J.A.D. (1972), 'Introduction', in R. Goodman, *After the
   Planners* (Harmondsworth, Penguin).

—— (1973), 'Planning and Community Work', *Journal of the Royal
   Town Planning Institutes,* vol.59, no.8, pp.352-3.

Panter-Brick (1953), 'Local Government and Democracy: a rejoinder',
   Public Administration, vol.31, pp.344-8.

Panter-Brick, K. (1954), 'Local Self-Government as a basis for
   democracy: a rejoinder', *Public Administration,* vol.32, pp.438-40.

Parker, J., and Allen, R. (1969), 'Social Workers in Local Government',
   Social and Economic Administration, vol.3, no.1, pp.17-38.

Parkinson, M. (1971), 'Central-Local Relations in British Parties: A
   Local View', *Political Studies,* vol.19, no.4, pp.440-6.

Parry, G. (1972), 'The Revolt against "Normal Politics"', *Government
   and Opposition,* vol.7, no.2, pp.145-52.

Pease, E. (1963), *History of the Fabian Society* (London, Frank Cass).

Peel, J. (1967), 'The West Riding County Council Election of 1958',
   South Western Review of Public Administration, no.3, pp.40-55.

Pelling, H.M. (1965), *The Origins of the Labour Party 1880-1900*
   (London, Oxford University Press).

P.E.P. (1947), 'Active Democracy – a local election', *Planning,* January.

—— (1948), 'Local elections: how many vote?', *Planning,* November.

—— (1955), 'Voting for local councils', *Planning,* May.

Perkin, H. (1973), 'Public Participation in Government Decision-making:
   the Historical Experience', *Procedings of the Town and Country
   Planning Summer School 1973* (London, Royal Town Planning
   Institute), pp.6-9.

Perkins, B., and Barnes, G. (1975), 'A Planning Choice', *Journal of the
   Royal Town Planning Institute,* vol.61, no.3, pp.96-8.

Peschek, D., and Brand, J. (1966), *Policies and Politics in Secondary
   Education,* Greater London Paper 11 (London, London School of
   Economics and Political Science).

Peterson, P.E. (1971), 'British Interest Group Theory Re-examined:
   The Politics of Comprehensive Education in Three British Cities',

Comparative Politics, vol.3, no.3, pp.381-402.

Petrie, C. (1972), *A Historian Looks at His World* (London, Sidgwick and Jackson).

Pimlott, B. (1972), 'Does Local Party Organisation Matter?', *British Journal of Political Science,* vol.2, no.3, pp.381-3.

—— (1973), 'Local Party Organisation, Turnout and Marginality', *British Journal of Political Science,* vol.3, no.2, pp.252-5.

Pinto-Duschinsky, M. (1972), 'Central Office and "Power" in the Conservative Party', *Political Studies,* vol.20, no.1, pp.1-16.

Poole, K.P. (1970), 'England and Wales', *Studies in Comparative Local Government,* vol.4, no.1, pp.7-19.

Popplestone, G. (1967), 'Conflict and Mediating Roles in Expanding Settlements', *Sociological Review,* vol.15, no.3, pp.339-55.

—— (1971), 'The Ideology of Professional Community Workers', *British Journal of Social Work,* vol.1, no.1, pp.85-104.

Potter, A.M. (1956), 'The English Conservative Constituency Association', *Western Political Quarterly,* vol.9, pp.363-75.

Price, C. (1971), 'Labour and the Town Halls', *New Statesman,* 2 July.

Pulzer, P.G.J. (1967), *Political Representation and Elections in Britain* (London, Allen and Unwin).

Ramsden, J., and Jay, R. (1973), 'Lincoln: Background to Taverne's Triumph', in C. Cook and J. Ramsden, *By-Elections in British Politics* (London, Macmillan).

Rankin, G. (1971), 'Professional Social Work and the Campaign against Poverty', *Social Work Today,* vol.1, no.10, pp.19-21.

Redcliffe-Maud, Lord, and Wood, B. (1974), *English Local Government Reformed* (London, Oxford University Press).

Rees, A.M., and Smith, T. (1964), *Town Councillors: A Study of Barking* (London, Acton Society Trust).

Regan, D.E., and Morris A.J.A. (1969), 'Local Government Corruption and Public Confidence', *Public Law,* pp.132-52.

Regan, T. (1968), 'Councillors Rarely Enter Parliament', *New Society,* 21 March.

Reid, J., and Richmond, S. (1974), *You Can't Judge a Book by Looking at the Cover* (Croydon, Suburban Press).

Rein, M. (1970), 'Social Work in Search of a Radical Profession', *Social Work,* vol.15, no.2, pp.13-28.

Rhodes, E.C. (1938a), 'The Exercise of the Franchise in London', *Political Quarterly,* vol.9, pp.113-19.

—— (1938b), 'Voting at Municipal Elections', *Political Quarterly,* vol.9, pp.271-80.

Rhodes, G. (ed.) (1972), *The New Government of London: the first five years* (London, Weidenfeld and Nicolson).

Rhodes, James, R. (1969), *Memoirs of a Conservative* (London, Weidenfeld and Nicolson).

Rhodes, R.A.W. (1971), 'Hinterland Politics', *British Journal of Political Science,* vol.1, no.1, pp.123-8.

Richardson, C. and Lethbridge, J. (1972), 'The Anti-Immigrant Vote in Bradford', *Race Today,* vol.4, no.4, pp.120-3.

Robbins, J.H.R. (1972), 'The Conservative intervention in Doncaster Borough politics', *British Journal of Political Science,* vol.2, no.4, pp.510-13.

Robertson, E. (1974), *The Local Radio Handbook* (London, Mowbrays).

Robson, W.A. (1931), 'Valediction', *Local Government News,* vol.VIII, no.10, December, pp.78-9.

—— (1966), 'Local Government in the Welfare State', *Political Quarterly,* vol.37, pp.121-7.

—— (1966), *Local Government in Crisis* (London, Allen and Unwin).

—— (1972), 'The Great City of Today', in W.A. Robson and D.E. Regan (eds.), *Great Cities of the World* (London, Allen and Unwin).

Rogaly, J. (1975), 'The Only Local Government We Can Afford', *Financial Times,* 4 February

Rose, R. (1962), 'The Political Ideals of English Party Activists', *American Political Science Review,* vol.56, no.2, pp.360-71.

—— (1969), 'The Variability of Party Government: A Theoretical and Empirical Critique', *Political Studies,* vol.17, no.4, pp.413-45.

—— (1974a), *Politics in England Today* (London, Faber and Faber).

—— (1974b), *The Problem of Party Government* (London, Macmillan).

—— (1974c), *Electoral Behaviour* (New York, Free Press).

Rossi, P.H., and Dentler, R.A. (1961), *The Politics of Urban Renewal* (New York, Free Press of Glencoe).

Rowley, G. (1971), 'The GLC Elections of 1964 and 1967: a study in electoral geography', *Transactions of the Institute of British Geographers,* vol.53, pp.117-31.

Royal Commission on the Constitution (1973), *Devolution and Other Aspects of Government: An Attitudes Survey,* Research Paper no.7, (London, HMSO).

Royal Commission on Local Government in England (1969), Research Studies 1. *Local Government in South East England;* Research Studies 2. *Lessons of the London Government Reforms;* Research Studies 9. *Community Attitudes Survey* (London, HMSO).

Royal Commission on Local Government in Scotland (1969), *Report and Appendices;* Research Study 2, *Community Survey: Scotland* (Edinburgh, HMSO).

Salvidge, S. (1934), *Salvidge of Liverpool* (London, Hodder and Stoughton).

Saran R. (1967), 'Decision Making by a Local Education Authority', *Public Administration,* vol.45, pp.387-402.

—— (1973), *Policy Making in Secondary Education* (London, Oxford University Press).

Savitch, H.V. (1973), 'Leadership and Decision-making in New York and London', *Policy and Politics,* vol.2, no.2, pp.113-34.

Scarrow, H.A. (1971), 'Policy Pressures by British Local Government: the case of Regulation in the "Public Interest"', *Comparative Politics,* vol.4, no.1, pp.1-28.

—— (1973), 'New Perspectives on British Local Government', *World Politics,* vol.26, no.1, pp.126-38.

Schattschneider, E.E. (1960), *The Semi-Sovereign People* (New York, Holt, Rinehart and Winston).

Scottish Development Department (1973), *The New Scottish Local Authorities: Organisation and Management Structures* (Edinburgh, HMSO).

Select Committee on Nationalised Industries (1971), *Relations with the Public,* Second Report, Session 1970-1, House of Commons Paper 514 (London, HMSO).

Self, P. (1971), 'Elected Representatives and Management in Local Authorities', *Public Administration,* vol.49, pp.269-77.

—— (1972), *Administrative Theories and Politics* (London, Allen and Unwin).

Seymour-Ure, C. (1974), *The Political Impact of Mass Media* (London, Constable).

Sharp, E. (1962), 'The Future of Local Government', *Public Administration,* vol.40, pp.375-86.

Sharpe, L.J. (1960), 'The Politics of Local Government in Greater London', *Public Administration,* vol.38, pp.157-72.

—— (1962a), *A Metropolis Votes,* Greater London Paper 8 (London, London School of Economics and Political Science).

—— (1962b), 'Elected Representatives in Local Government', *British Journal of Sociology,* vol.13, no.3, pp.169-209.

—— (1965), *Why Local Democracy?,* Fabian Tract 361 (London, Fabian Society).

—— (1966), 'Leadership and Representation in Local Government', *Political Quarterly,* vol.37, pp.149-58.

—— (ed.) (1967), *Voting in Cities* (London, Macmillan).

—— (1970), 'Theories and Values of Local Government', *Political Studies*, vol.18, no.2, pp.153-74.

—— (1973), 'American Democracy Reconsidered', *British Journal of Political Science*, vol.3, nos.1 and 2, pp.1-28 and 129-68.

Sheehan, J.J. (1971), 'Liberalism and the City in Germany', *Past and Present*, no.51, pp.116-37.

Sheffield Trades and Labour Council (1967), *Forty Years of Labour Rule in Sheffield* (Sheffield, STLC).

Sherman, A. (1970), 'The End of Local Government?', in R. Boyson (ed.), *Right Turn* (London, Churchill Press) pp.117-37.

Simmie, J.M. (1974), *Citizens in Conflict* (London, Hutchinson).

Simon, S. (1938), *A Century of City Government* (London, Allen and Unwin).

Smallwood, F. (1965), *Greater London: the politics of metropolitan reform* (New York, Bobbs-Merrill).

Smith, C.S., and Anderson, B. (1972), 'Political Participation through Community Action', in G. Parry (ed.), *Participation in Politics* (Manchester, Manchester University Press).

Smith, F.H. (1944), 'The Expert in the Local Government Service', *Public Administration*, vol.22, pp.30-40.

Smith, T.D. (1965), 'Local Government in Newcastle: the background to some recent developments', *Public Administration*, vol.43, pp.413-18.

—— (1970), *An Autobiography* (Newcastle, Oriel Press).

Solesbury, W. (1974), *Policy in Urban Planning* (Oxford, Pergamon).

Spencer, P. (1971), 'Party Politics and the Processes of Local Democracy in an English Town Council', in A. Richards and A. Kuper, *Councils in Action* (London, Cambridge University Press).

Spiers, M., and Lelohe, M.J. (1964), 'Pakistanis in the Bradford Municipal Elections of 1963', *Political Studies*, vol.12, no.1, pp.85-92.

Stacey, F. (1971), *The British Ombudsman* (London, Oxford University Press).

Stacey, M. (1960), *Tradition and Change* (London, Oxford University Press).

——, Batston, E., Bell, C., and Murcott, A. (1975), *Power, Persistence and Change* (London, Routledge).

Stack, H.J. (1970), 'Grass-roots militants and Ideology', *Polity*, vol.2, no.4, pp.426-42.

Stanyer, J. (1967a), 'The Maud Committee Report: a critical review', *Social and Economic Administration*, vol.1, no.4, pp.3-19.

—— (1967b), *County Government in England and Wales* (London, Routledge).

—— (1970a), 'Electoral Behaviour in Local Government: A Model of a Two-Party System', *Political Studies,* vol.18, no.2, pp.187-204.

—— (1970b), 'A Theoretical Analysis of Local Support for National Political Parties', *Political Studies,* vol.18, no.3, pp.395-9.

—— (1970c), 'Social and Rational Models of Man: Alternative Approaches to the Study of Local Elections', *Advancement of Science,* vol.26, no.130, pp.399-407.

—— (1971a), 'Why Does Local Turnout Vary?', *New Society,* 13 May.

—— (1971b), 'Elected Representatives and Management in Local Authorities', *Public Administration,* vol.49, pp.73-97.

Steed, M. (1965), 'The Independent Councillors', *Insight,* April, pp.13-17.

—— (1966), 'Local Elections: Variability and Comparability', *Insight,* June, pp.6-11.

—— (1967), 'A New Life for Local Politics', *New Society,* 28 December.

—— (1969), 'The Maud Report Examined – Politics: More Balance?', *New Society,* 19 June.

Stewart, J.D. (1973a), 'Developments in Corporate Planning in British Local Government: The Bains Report and Corporate Planning', *Local Government Studies,* no.5, pp.13-29.

—— (1973b), *Management – Local – Environment – Urban – Government: Some Words Considered,* An Inaugural Lecture (Birmingham, University of Birmingham).

—— (1974), 'The Politics of Local Government Reorganisation', in K. Jones (ed.), *The Year Book of Social Policy in Britain, 1973* (London, Routledge), pp.21-33.

Swaffield, J.C. (1960), 'Green Fingers in the Council Chamber', *Public Administration,* vol.38, pp.131-6.

Taras, R. (1972), 'Communications and Press Relations in Urban Government', *Policy and Politics,* vol.1, no.2, pp.115-30.

Taylor, A.H. (1972), 'The Effect of Party Organisation: Correlation between Campaign Expenditure and Voting in the 1970 Election', *Political Studies,* vol.20, no.3, pp.329-31.

Thornhill, W. (1957), 'Agreements between Political Parties in Local Government Matters', *Political Studies,* vol.5, no.1, pp.83-8.

Todd, N. (1975), 'The Uses of Contemporary Suburban History', *Local Historian,* vol.11, no.5, pp.285-9.

TUC (1973), 'TUC Regional Organisation', *Report of 105th Annual Conference of the Trades Union Congress,* Annex A, pp.356-76.

Tunstall, J. (1970), *The Westminster Lobby Correspondents* (London,

Routledge).

Turner, N.G. (1973), *Community Radio in Britain: a practical introduction* (London, Whole Earth Tools).

Van Til, J., and S.B. (1970), 'Citizen Participation in Social Policy: the End of the Cycle?', *Social Problems*, vol.17, no.3, pp.313-23.

Vickers, G. (1974), 'Policy Making in Local Government', *Local Government Studies*, no.7, pp.5-12.

Wahlke, J., Eulau, H., Buchanan, W., and Ferguson, L.C. (1952), *The Legislative System* (New York, Wiley).

Walsh, A.H. (1969), *The Urban Challenge to Government* (New York, Praeger).

Ward, C. (1974), *Tenants Take Over* (London, Architectural Press).

Warren, J.H. (1950), 'Local self-government: the basis of a democratic state', *Public Administration*, vol.28, pp.11-16.

——, and Richards, P.G. (1965), *The English Local Government System* (London, Allen and Unwin).

Webb, S., and B. (1963), *English Local Government: Volume 1 – The Parish and the County* (London, Frank Cass).

Weightman, G. (1974), 'Liberalpool in trouble', *New Society*, 12 September.

Wheare, K.C. (1955), *Government by Committee* (London, Oxford University Press).

Wickwar, W.H. (1970), *The Political Theory of Local Government* (Columbia, University of South Carolina Press).

Wiggins, D. (1971), 'The revolt in the cities', *The Times*, 3 April.

Wildavsky, A. (1966), 'The Political Economy of Efficiency', *Public Administration Review*, vol.26, pp.292-310.

Williams, J.E. (1955), 'Paternalism in Local Government in the 19th Century', *Public Administration*, vol.33, pp.439-46.

Williams, O.P. (1971), *Metropolitan Political Analysis* (New York, Free Press).

Willmott, P., and Young, M. (1960), *Family and Class in a London Suburb* (London, Routledge).

Wilson, D.J. (1972), 'Party bureaucracy in Britain: regional and area organisation', *British Journal of Political Science*, vol.2, no.3, pp.373-81.

—— (1973), 'Constituency Party Autonomy and Central Control', *Political Studies*, vol.21, no.2, pp.167-74.

Wiseman, H.V. (1963a), 'The Party Caucus in local government', *New Society*, 31 October.

—— (1963b), 'The Working of Local Government in Leeds', *Public*

Administration, vol.41, pp.51-69 and 137-55.

—— (1967), *Local Government at Work* (London, Routledge).

Wistrich, E. (1972), *Local Government Reorganisation: the first years of Camden* (London, London Borough of Camden).

Woodham, J.B. (1972), 'Management and Local Democracy', *Local Government Studies,* no.2, pp.13-21.

Worple, K., and Hudson, R. (1970), 'Community Press', *New Society,* 24 September.

Worcester, R. (1972), 'The Hidden Activists', *New Society,* 8 June.

Yearley, C.K. (1973), 'The "Provincial Party" and the Megalopolises: London, Paris and New York, 1850-1910', *Comparative Studies in Social History,* vol.15, pp.51-88.

Young, K. (1973), 'The Politics of London Government 1880-1899', *Public Administration,* vol.51, pp.91-108.

—— (1973), 'Orpington and the "Liberal Revival"', in C. Cook and J. Ramsden, *By-Elections in British Politics* (London, Macmillan).

Zisk, B.H., Eulau, H., and Prewitt, K. (1965), 'City councilmen and the group struggle: a typology of role orientations', *Journal of Politics,* vol.27, pp.618-46.

2. Interviews

1. Leonard Allen, Local Government Officer, Conservative Central Office.
2. Arthur Blenkinsop, MP, Chairman of the Planning and Local Government Group of the Parliamentary Labour Party.
3. Herbert Brabin, former Local Government Officer (1946-63), Conservative Central Office.
4. Ann Carlton, former Local Government Officer (1965-74), the Labour Party.
5. John Cartwright MP, Chairman of the Regional and Local Government Sub-Committee of the Labour Party National Executive.
6. Horace Cutler, Leader of the Conservative Party, Greater London Council.
7. Cecil Dawson, former Local Government Officer (1963-74), Conservative Central Office.
8. Jeremy Eccles, Local Government Correspondent, BBC Radio London.
9. Stephen Haseler, Chairman (1973-5) General Purposes Committee, Greater London Council.
10. Arthur Jones MP, former Chairman (1963-73) of the Conservative Party National Advisory Committee on Local Government.
11. Ed Miller, Local Government Officer, the Labour Party.

12. Peter Redhouse, Deputy General Manager, BBC Local Radio.
13. Reg Underhill, National Agent of the Labour Party.
14. Peter Walker, Councillor, London Borough of Croydon; Head of the Private Office of the Leader of the Greater London Council.
15. Dick Wilson, Leader of the Nottinghamshire County Council.

3. Other Sources

1. Minutes of the National Executive Committee of the Labour Party.
2. Papers of Mr Herbert Brabin, including local election statistics prepared by Conservative Central Office.
3. Minutes of the Nottinghamshire Temporary Co-ordinating Committee of the Labour Party.

INDEX

188